Questions in
Standard Grade
Home Economics

Alastair MacGregor

Text © 2003 Alastair MacGregor
Design and layout © 2003 Leckie & Leckie Ltd

Cover image © DAVID MUNNS/SCIENCE PHOTO LIBRARY

02/240407

ISBN 978-1-84372-074-4

Published by
Leckie & Leckie Ltd, 3rd floor, 4 Queen Street, Edinburgh, EH2 1JE
Tel: 0131 220 6831 Fax: 0131 225 9987
enquiries@leckieandleckie.co.uk   www.leckieandleckie.co.uk

Edited by Margaret Wilson

Special thanks to Simon Appleford (page make up), Bruce Ryan (project management), Finola Stack (illustration)

A CIP Catalogue record for this book is available from the British Library.

Leckie & Leckie Ltd is a division of Huveaux plc.

Contents

Leckie & Leckie would like to thank the Scottish Qualifications Authority for permission to reproduce extracts from the 2001 Standard Grade Home Economics General Level exam. The SQA is not responsible for any answers provided in this book.
Leckie & Leckie acknowledges that all trademarks used in this book are the property of their owners.

Introduction

The questions and information in this book will help to prepare you for your Standard Grade Home Economics exam.

The Standard Grade Home Economics assessment includes:
- a written examination;
- a variety of practical exercises;
- at least two Practical Assignments.

This book will help you prepare for all **three** areas.

The Standard Grade Home Economics course has three assessable elements:

- Knowledge and Understanding (KU): assessed in the written examination;
- Handling Information (HI): assessed in the written examination;
- Practical and Organisational Skills (P&OS): assessed in the Practical Exercise and the Practical Assignment.

The questions in this book cover the range of essential knowledge statements for the course. The questions cover both KU and HI. The questions are structured to cover Foundation, General and Credit Levels.

The book uses a key to indicate which questions are **KU** and which questions are **HI**.

Answers are provided in the pull out section.

You should attempt all the questions in this book, using Leckie & Leckie's *Standard Grade Home Economics Course Notes*.

At the top of each section of questions, you will find references to Leckie & Leckie's *Standard Grade Home Economics Course Notes*. Study these pages before you answer the questions.

Use a jotter or paper for your answers. You may need a ruler for drawing tables.

The remaining sections in the book cover the element of Practical and Organisational Skills. These sections provide you with step by step instructions on how to plan a Practical Exercise and carry out the Practical Assignment.

Leckie & Leckie

Exam
Technique

The Standard Grade Home Economics exam assesses Knowledge and Understanding and Handling Information at Foundation, General and Credit levels. The following pages provide you with information that will help you when preparing for the exam. The information will also be very useful when answering the questions in this book.

Knowledge and Understanding

In this type of question you have to either recall or use your knowledge of Home Economics. In each question paper you will definitely be asked to recall and use your knowledge of nutrition and healthy eating.

Look at the example below:

1. (a) Soup is a popular dish in the Scottish diet.

SCOTCH BROTH

INGREDIENTS
Meat Stock, Barley,
Dried Peas, Carrots,
Turnip, Onion,
Leek, Parsley,

Identify **three** of the Scottish dietary targets to which Scotch Broth would contribute.

For **each** target, give a **different** benefit to health.

Target **Double intake of fruit and vegetables**

Benefit to health **Provides NSP, which can help prevent constipation**

Target **Reduce salt intake**

Benefit to health **Will help to prevent high blood pressure; there is no salt added**

Target **Sugar intake to be reduced by adults and children**

Benefit to health **Will help prevent tooth decay and obesity as there is no added sugar**

	Marks	KU	HI
	(1)	1	
	(1)	1	
	(1)	1	
	(1)	1	
	(1)	1	
	(1)	1	

Leckie & Leckie

It is important that you read the question carefully.

The right hand column tells you that this is a KU question worth six marks.

Three marks are awarded for identifying three different dietary targets and three marks for giving a reason how each target can benefit health.

You should start by underlining or highlighting the important parts of the question.

You will need to use your knowledge of the Scottish dietary targets to answer this question. In this example, the candidate has given three different and correct targets.

You will also need to use your knowledge of nutrition to answer the question. The candidate has then given three correct benefits to health for each of the targets.

If the question had asked you to give the benefits to the health of a pregnant woman, you would have to make sure your answer referred to a pregnant woman.

Handling Information

In this type of question you are usually given a case study and a chart of information.

You have to read the case study carefully and then select the best product or service from the chart.

Look at the example below:

It is important that you read the question carefully.

1. **(continued)**

    (c) A young enterprise group is selling soup to support their school's healthy eating campaign.

    The containers for the soup must be

    - safe
    - inexpensive
    - easy to store.

    Study the information about soup containers shown below.

	INFORMATION ABOUT SOUP CONTAINERS					
Container	*Made from*	*Cost*	*Size*	*Rigidity*	*Insulating properties*	*Special features*
A	China	£1·50 each ✗	large	**** ✓	*** ✓	• Narrow top ✗ • Healthy eating logo ✓
B	Polystyrene	2p ✓ each	medium	*** ✓	***** ✓	• Wide top ✓ • Non-spill lid ✓ • Stackable ✓
C	Waxed paper	1p ✓ each	small	** ✗	** ✗	• Slimline ✗ • Stackable ✓
D	Plastic	1p ✓ each	medium	** ✗	** ✗	• Slimline ✗ • Non-spill lid ✓ • Stackable ✓

Key: ***** good ⟶ * poor

Leckie & Leckie

1. *(c)* **(continued)**

Which container would be the **most suitable** for serving soup?

Soup container   *B*_____   ① | | 1

Give **three** reasons for your choice.

1 The school needs the containers to be stackable to make them easy to store. This container is stackable.

① | | 1

2 This container has good insulating properties, keeping the soup hot, but the outside of the container cool; it is therefore safe to use.

① | | 1

3 The container has a wide top, which makes it easier to fill with soup, making it safe for the pupils to use.

① | | 1

The right hand side column tells you that this is a HI question worth 4 marks.

One mark is for identifying the most suitable product and three marks are for your reason for choosing this product.

You should start by <u>underlining</u> or highlighting the important parts of the case study.

You then look at the chart of information to select the correct product. You should look through each product to see if it meets the needs of the case study.

The container needs to be inexpensive. This rules out container A.

The container needs to be easy to stack. This rules out container A.

The container needs to be safe. Containers C and D are ruled out because they have poor insulating properties, i.e. the containers will get hot, and they are not rigid, making them both difficult and unsafe to hold.

This leaves container B as the one that meets the criteria of being safe, inexpensive and easy to store.

In this example the candidate has indicated with a tick and a cross which features of each container meet the needs of the school. Only container B has all ticks.

Leckie & Leckie

Questions

Eating a variety of foods contributes to health

See pages 11–17 of Leckie & Leckie's *Standard Grade Home Economics Course Notes.*

KU **Question 1**

The following foods are found in the snack lunch box of an eight-year-old child:

- orange;

- carton of semi-skimmed milk;

- wholemeal sandwich with chicken, tomato and cucumber;

- chocolate covered raisins.

(*a*)   List **six** nutrients that can be found in this lunch.

(*b*)   List the food(s) in which you would find **each** nutrient.

(*c*)   Explain why **each** nutrient is important for the health of an eight-year-old child.

KU **Question 2**

(*a*)   List **three** antioxidant vitamins.

(*b*)   Explain the function of antioxidants in the body.

KU **Question 3**

Fruit and vegetables are a good source of water and Non-starch Polysaccharides (NSP).

Explain **two** benefits to health of ensuring:

(*a*)   a regular intake of water;

(*b*)   a regular intake of NSP.

KU **Question 4**

The following ingredients are combined in a meal:

- liver and orange juice;

- milk and cheese;

- spinach and milk.

Thinking about the inter-relationship of nutrients, explain the possible nutritional effects of **each** combination.

KU   Question 5

Copy and complete **each** of the flow diagrams below to show the different classifications and sources of proteins, carbohydrates and fats.

(a)

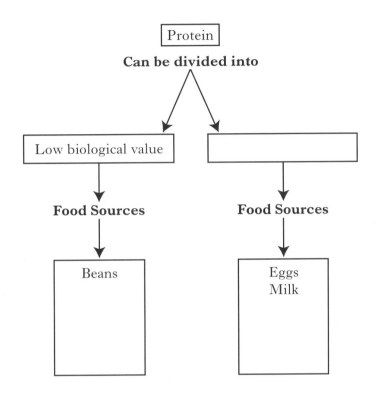

(b)

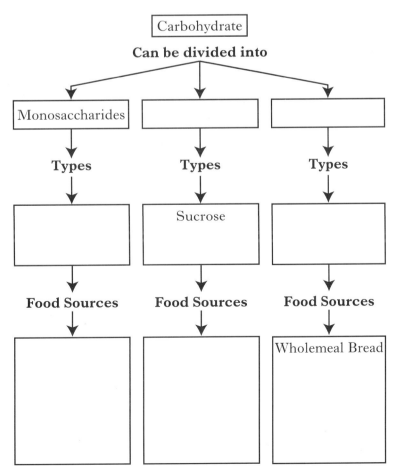

(c)

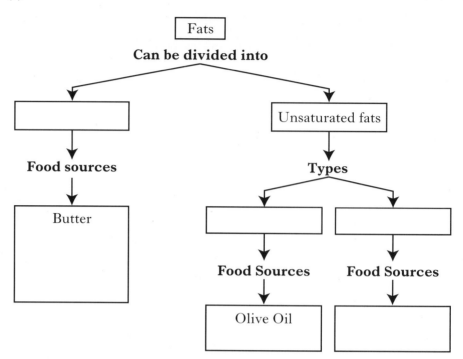

Question 6

Study the information about the following chocolate drinks:

Drink	kJ/calories per cup	Fat per cup
Malted Chocolate Drink	1·56 / 373	1·7g
Choco Drink	1·60 / 381	4·7g
Choco 'Light' Drink	1·58 / 378	4·1g
MaltoChoc Drink	1·51 / 360	1·9g
MaltoChoc 'Light' Drink	1·50 / 358	5·9g
Chocolate Drink	1·72 / 411	12·2g

(a)   Which drink contains the most fat per cup?

(b)   Which drink contains the least kJ/calories per cup?

(c)   Which drink would be the most suitable for a person on a low fat diet?

KU
KU   (d)   What is surprising about the energy and fat content of the MaltoChoc drinks?

(e)   List **one** function of fat in the diet.

Current dietary advice

See pages 21–28 of Leckie & Leckie's *Standard Grade Home Economics Course Notes*.

KU **Question 7**

Study the menu below:

Menu

Carrot and coriander soup
Home made bread
Tuna and wholemeal pasta bake
Fresh fruit kebab served with low fat yoghurt

(*a*)   List **six** different dietary targets to which this menu can contribute.

(*b*)   Explain how the menu contributes to **each** of the dietary targets you have listed.

KU **Question 8**

Study the menu below:

Menu

Cream of tomato soup served with a white bread roll
Deep fried battered salmon strips served with garlic mayonnaise dip
Baked potato and butter with green salad
Fresh fruit salad in a light syrup, served with ice cream

(*a*)   List **five** changes that could be made to the menu to help meet dietary targets.

(*b*)   Explain your reasons for making **each** change.

KU **Question 9**

Explain how **each** of the following methods of cooking can contribute to a healthy diet:

(*a*)   steaming;

(*b*)   stir frying;

(*c*)   microwave cooking.

Question 10

Explain the effects of **each** of the following on health:

(a)   an excess of fat in the diet;

(b)   a lack of NSP in the diet;

(c)   a lack of folic acid in the diet.

HI   **Question 11**

As part of a healthy eating programme, Sandy is deciding on which type of bread he should eat.

Study the information on breads below:

INFORMATION ON BREADS				
Bread type	*NSP content per slice*	*Salt content per slice*	*Fat content per slice*	*Additional information*
A	1·25 g	137·5 mg	0·55 kJ	Made with organic flour
B	1·75 g	70.0 mg	0·75 kJ	Added germ makes this rich in iron
C	1·00 g	135·0 mg	0·42 kJ	Enriched with folic acid
D	2·25 g	70·0 mg	0·40 kJ	No added fat or sugar

(a)   (i)   Which bread best suits the needs of Sandy?
       (ii) Give **three** reasons for your answer.

(b)   Which bread would be most suitable for a couple planning for a baby?

(c)   Which bread would be most suitable for a person suffering from anaemia?

(d)   Which bread would be most suitable for someone who is concerned about the environment?

(e)   Give a reason for **each** of your answers above.

(f)   What symbol might you find on bread type A?

Leckie & Leckie

KU **Question 12**

Study the information below:

LATE NIGHT TAKEAWAY CURRY	LOAD UP PLAN		
Consists of	*Consists of*		
• Chicken Korma • Fried Rice • Naan Bread	Breakfast: • Grilled rasher of bacon • Grilled reduced fat sausage • 2 grilled mushrooms • Grilled tomato • Poached egg on toast	Lunch: • Banana • Apple • Digestive biscuit	Evening meal: • Ready-made chicken curry • Can cola
Contains: 6240 kJ 85 g fat	*Contains:* 5860 kJ 36 g fat		

Explain why the load up plan would be a better health choice than the late night takeaway curry.

Individuals have varying dietary needs

See pages 31–38 of Leckie & Leckie's *Standard Grade Home Economics Course Notes*.

HI **Question 13**

Taking account of the Dietary Reference Values for males aged 11–14 years old, evaluate the suitability of the day's meals for an overweight 12-year-old male:

DIETARY ANALYSIS OF A DAY'S MEALS					
Energy kJ per day	*Protein* g per day	*Iron* mg per day	*Calcium* mg per day	*Vitamin C* mg per day	*Sodium* mg per day
3800	56·0	8·3	1002	20	2500

DIETARY REFERENCE VALUES FOR MALES AGED 11–14					
Estimated Average Requirement (EAR)	*Reference Nutrient Intakes (RNI)*				
Energy kJ per day	*Protein* g per day	*Iron* mg per day	*Calcium* mg per day	*Vitamin C* mg per day	*Sodium* mg per day
2200	42·1	11·3	1000	35	1600

KU **Question 14**

Study the foods shown in the picture below.

(a) Which of the foods shown would be **unsuitable** for a:

  • lacto vegetarian;

  • vegan;

  • pregnant woman.

(b) Explain why **each** would be unsuitable.

KU Question 15

Explain why exposure to sunlight might be important for a vegan.

HI Question 16

Taking account of the Dietary Reference Values for females aged 50+ years, evaluate the suitability of the day's meals for a 66-year-old female suffering from constipation.

DIETARY ANALYSIS OF A DAY'S MEALS					
Energy kJ per day	NSP g per day	Vitamin B1 mg per day	Calcium mg per day	Vitamin D μg per day	Protein g per day
3800	8	1·0	500	6	36·5

DIETARY REFERENCE VALUES FOR FEMALES AGED 50+ YEARS					
Estimated Average Requirement (EAR)		Reference Nutrient Intakes (RNI)			
Energy kJ per day	NSP g per day	Vitamin B1 mg per day	Calcium mg per day	Vitamin D μg per day	Protein g per day
1900	18 (approx)	0·8	700	10	46·5

Cleanliness is important in relation to health

See pages 41–56 of Leckie & Leckie's *Standard Grade Home Economics Course Notes*.

KU **Question 17**

The following symbols appear on a jacket:

Describe how you would launder this garment.

KU **Question 18**

A chef has a 100% white cotton overall with no special finishes.

Copy out the chart below and draw the care label symbols that you would expect to see on this garment.

Washing symbol	Ironing symbol	Drying symbol	Bleaching symbol	Dry cleaning symbol

KU **Question 19**

Read the case study below and answer the questions that follow.

A Home Economics student was preparing foods for a summer buffet. Because the room was warm, he left the window open to let in cool air. The student was suffering from hayfever and was constantly sneezing when preparing the food.

The student had forgotten his apron and so tied a drying cloth round his waist. He later used the cloth for drying dishes. One of the foods had to be served cold so the student placed the hot food into the refrigerator to cool quickly.

(a) List **two** ways in which the student has broken:

- personal hygiene rules;

- kitchen hygiene rules.

(b) Explain the possible consequences of breaking **each** rule.

KU Question 20

Explain what is meant by the term 'danger zone'.

KU Question 21

A pot of lentil soup has been left in a warm kitchen for 36 hours. The soup has to be thrown out because it has a layer of mould on top and has a sour smell.

Explain how **each** of the following factors might have contributed to the spoilage of the soup:

- temperature;
- food;
- moisture;
- oxygen;
- pH.

KU Question 22

(a) Following a successful summer harvest, a gardener wishes to preserve some produce for use in winter. He has the following produce:

- apples;
- peas;
- onions;
- strawberries;
- cauliflower;
- cabbage;
- plums;
- brussel sprouts.

Copy and complete the chart below to show how **each** product could be preserved.

Remember that some products can be preserved by more than one method.

Freezing	Pickling / chutney making	Jam making	Chilling	Vacuum packing

(b) The gardener has been given three fresh trout by a friend. He is going to freeze the trout so he can use them in the winter.

  (i) Explain why freezing trout will make them last for a longer period of time.

  (ii) List **three** points that the gardener would have to consider when selecting the **packaging** to use for freezing the trout.

(c) The gardener has decided to freeze a large quantity of raspberries. He plans to use small quantities of raspberries throughout the winter months.

List **five** points, **other than packaging materials**, that he would have to consider to ensure that the raspberries remain in good condition until their eventual use.

KU   **Question 23**

List **five** possible symptoms of food poisoning.

KU   **Question 24**

A student was preparing the evening meal for friends.

Read the list of actions that took place whilst she was preparing and cooking the meal.

Action 1   The chicken was not fully defrosted, but it was going to cook in the oven for $1^{1}/_{2}$ hours so she thought this would be all right.

Action 2   The chicken was sitting on a plastic chopping board that was later used to chop vegetables for a salad.

Action 3   The cheesecake had not fully defrosted so it was left to defrost by the open window.

Explain the possible outcome of **each** action listed above.

KU   **Question 25**

(*a*)   Study the picture below.

Explain why the picture **does not** demonstrate good food storage.

(*b*)   Explain why a refrigerator should be regularly cleaned.

(*c*)   Explain why a freezer should be regularly defrosted.

See pages 59–64 (and page 95 for Question 28b) of
Leckie & Leckie's *Standard Grade Home Economics Course Notes*.

KU **Question 26**

Study each of the pictures below.

For **each** picture identify:

    (*a*)   **One** possible safety hazard;

    (*b*)   The type of accident it might cause;

    (*c*)   What action could be taken to prevent the accident.

KU **Question 27**

Explain why the elderly and the young are most at risk from household accidents.

KU **Question 28**

    (*a*)   A school has bought some electric blenders for use in the Home Economics Department.

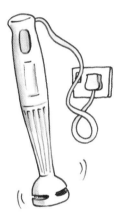

        List **five** rules that should be followed by the pupils to make sure the blenders are used safely.

    (*b*)   The symbol shown below appears on the electric blenders.

        What information does this symbol give to the consumer?

Design features

See pages 67–78 of Leckie & Leckie's *Standard Grade Home Economics Course Notes*.

KU **Question 29**

A single parent is planning to buy a pair of jeans for his 16-year-old daughter's birthday.

List and explain **four** factors that he would need to consider before purchasing the jeans.

KU **Question 30**

A couple is buying a new outfit for their 6 month old baby.

Study the information below:

Outfit:

Design features:

- 3-piece outfit comprising trousers, T-shirt and cardigan;
- cotton fleece type T-shirt with press stud fastening at shoulder;
- Printed logo on T-shirt;
- Fleece type zip front cardigan with hood;
- Fleece type trousers with elasticated waist;
- Inverted pleats on the trouser knees;
- Colours: pale blue and cream/pale green and cream/pale pink and cream;
- Sizes: 1 month, 3 month, 6 month, 9 month and 12 month.

Choose **six** design features and explain why **each** would be suitable for the baby.

KU   Question 31

The chef in a café, that has a large number of student customers, is buying a new pair of chef trousers.

Evaluate the suitability of the trousers shown below.

Trousers:

Design features:

- 100% cotton designer baggies;
- Extra soft finish;
- Two side pockets and one back pocket;
- Tapered legs;
- Elasticated waist with drawstring;
- Available in 6 different fabric designs;
- Available with special flame-resistant finish.

KU   Question 32

(*a*)   List **six** different energy saving measures that you could take when using:

   (i)   an electric washing machine OR
   (ii)   an electric dishwasher.

(*b*)   Explain why **each** measure might save energy.

KU   Question 33

Study the design features of the kettle below:

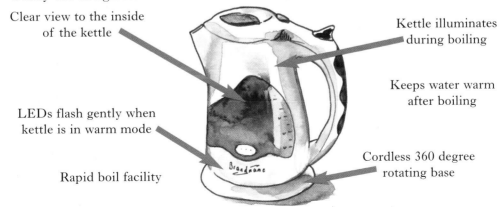

Clear view to the inside of the kettle

Kettle illuminates during boiling

Keeps water warm after boiling

LEDs flash gently when kettle is in warm mode

Rapid boil facility

Cordless 360 degree rotating base

Explain why this kettle might be suitable for:

(*a*)   someone who has hearing difficulties;

(*b*)   use in a small office.

Question 34

(a) The Home Economics Department is planning to buy a tumble dryer. It will be used daily for drying dish-cloths and dish towels. The Home Economics Department has a limited budget. Both staff and pupils will use the tumble dryer. The tumble drier will be placed against an internal wall near an available power socket at the back of a classroom.

Study the information on tumble dryers in the chart below:

INFORMATION ON TUMBLE DRYERS			
	Model A	*Model B*	*Model C*
Type *	Condenser	Condenser	Ducted
Cost	£129·90	£110·71	£89·53
Fuel used	Electricity	Electricity	Electricity & gas
Drying capacity	5 kg	6 kg	3 kg
Heat settings	1	2	2
Drying time	120 minutes	100 minutes	120 minutes
Noise level	Medium	Low	Medium
Energy rating	D	C	D
Colour	White	White	Cream
Filter	Access from back	Access from front	Access from side
Additional information	• Extended guarantee available • Free pack of fabric conditioner sheets	• Final cool tumble ** • Reverse action drying ***	• Final cool tumble ** • Extended guarantee available

* Using a condenser dryer allows you to fit your dryer almost anywhere in a room as moisture is removed and stored in a container within the machine that must be emptied occasionally. A ducted dryer requires an outside wall and a vent.

** Temperature reduces for the last 10 minutes of drying time preventing excess creasing.

*** Drum alternates between forward and reverse movements to speed up drying time and prevent tangling.

Choose the tumble dryer **most suited** to the needs of the Home Economics Department and give **eight different** reasons for your choice.

(b) Which tumble dryer would be the **most suitable** for a single man with a limited income?

HI   **Question 35**

A group of four students sharing a flat are putting money together to buy a new ironing board. Two of the students are starting a summer work placement in a local hotel and they have to wear shirts whilst on duty.

They are looking for an ironing board that is:
- easy to store;
- durable;
- suits different heights;
- inexpensive.

Study the information about ironing boards below:

INFORMATION ABOUT IRONING BOARDS			
	Ironing Board 1	*Ironing Board 2*	*Ironing Board 3*
Solid steel top *			YES
Mesh top **	YES	YES	
Size	95cm × 30cm	122cm × 43cm	96cm × 37cm
Height adjustable	No	No	Yes
Folded height	131cm	133cm	132cm
Manufacturer's guarantee on frame	5 years	10 years	10 years
Price	£12·99	£29·99	£17·99
Additional features	• Free replacement cover	• Movable/removable iron rest	• Free sleeve board

*   Solid steel top gives durability and strength.

**   Mesh top allows steam to pass through the board, keeping the surface dry.

Choose the **most suitable** ironing board for the students and give **four** different reasons for your choice.

HI **Question 36**

Sandy is a young woman who is starting up her own ironing business. She is planning to buy an iron that she will use in the business. She has been given a £400 start-up grant for equipment.

Evaluate the suitability of the iron below for use in the business.

£198·00

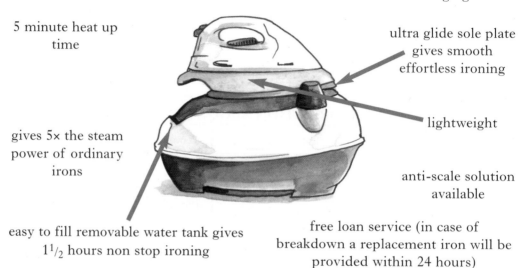

vertical steam for hanging fabrics

5 minute heat up time

ultra glide sole plate gives smooth effortless ironing

lightweight

gives 5× the steam power of ordinary irons

anti-scale solution available

easy to fill removable water tank gives 1½ hours non stop ironing

free loan service (in case of breakdown a replacement iron will be provided within 24 hours)

KU **Question 37**

What are the benefits of adding elastane fibres to a swimming costume?

KU **Question 38**

Copy and complete the fibre information chart below.

FIBRE INFORMATION CHART					
Fibre	*Natural or synthetic?*	*Strong or weak?*	*Flammable or non-flammable?*	*Absorbent or non-absorbent?*	*Easy or difficult to wash?*
Cotton					
Nylon					
Wool					
Silk					
Elastane					

Physical needs of individuals and families

See pages 81–98 of Leckie & Leckie's *Standard Grade Home Economics Course Notes*.

KU Question 39

The jacket shown below has been ordered for a mechanic who is called out to undertake roadside repairs on cars and lorries.

Read the details about the jacket:

Based on a unique design, the garment consists of two advanced fabric layers, a highly breathable, waterproof microporous liner with a completely detachable high-visibility outer.

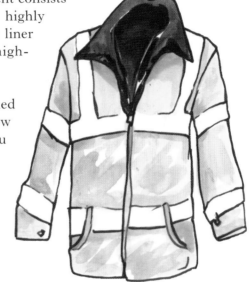

The garment can be regularly washed at 80°C, so that the bright yellow colour does not fade, keeping you looking good and safe.

The detachable high-visibility outer can be worn as a stand-alone, comfortable, summer jacket during hot, dry weather or worn with the microporous liner to provide the ultimate in wet weather protection.

Sew your existing badges onto the outer, to give you the most comfortable high-visibility jacket available.

The jacket features two large outer pockets and two internal zipped pockets. The jacket comes to upper thigh level, has adjustable Velcro® fastenings on the cuffs and a Velcro® front closing.

   (*a*)   Explain why this jacket would be suitable for a roadside mechanic.

   (*b*)   What **other** features could be added to the jacket to make it even more suitable for use?

   (*c*)   Explain your reason(s) for **each** added feature.

KU **Question 40**

A designer is thinking about some new trouser designs for a toddler. Explain why **each** of the following factors would need to be considered:

(*a*)   fastenings;

(*b*)   size;

(*c*)   absorbency;

(*d*)   stretch;

(*e*)   safety.

KU **Question 41**

Match **each** of the following forms of shelter to each of the groups given below:

A   Single man who works in a city centre bank.

B   A family consisting of a mother, father, 16-year-old boy and 14-year-old girl who have two dogs.

C   Person on a walking holiday who will be staying in remote areas of the countryside.

D   A criminal.

E   Family on a summer holiday to Spain.

F   An elderly couple with mobility problems.

KU **Question 42**

Read the situations below and decide which consumer organisation would provide the best advice:

(a) A consumer has fallen into debt with a variety of credit card companies.

(b) A consumer purchased a fish supper, but when he got home he discovered that the fish was mouldy underneath the batter.

(c) A consumer wishes to buy a new washing machine, but is confused by the wide range of models available.

(d) A consumer has received a letter from the local authority telling her that she is in rent arrears.

(e) A consumer has noisy neighbours who play loud music until the early hours of the morning.

(f) A consumer is concerned about the number of dogs fouling in the local park.

(g) A consumer is concerned about the sale of fireworks to young children in a local shop.

(h) A school wants to receive a talk from an expert in food safety.

(i) A consumer is concerned about the storage of gas canisters at a local garage.

(j) A consumer wishes to have assistance when writing a will.

(k) A consumer is looking for advice on the best type of bottled water to buy.

(l) A consumer is concerned about the standard of work carried out by a local plumber.

(m) A consumer wishes to get more information about a recent Scottish report on traffic congestion.

Consumer organisations:
- Citizen's Advice Bureau;
- Consumer Advice Centre;
- Consumers' Association;
- Consumer Protection Department;
- Environmental Health Department;
- Scottish Consumer Council.

Question 43

The trials and tribulations of Mr Smith.

Read the situations below and for **each** one:

    (*a*)   Identify which Act or regulation protects the consumer.

    (*b*)   Explain how the Act or regulation protects the consumer.

(Remember the consumer may be protected by more than one Act or regulation).

Situation 1
Mr Smith bought a trolley type suitcase for use on his short holiday to Italy. The first time he used it the wheels fell off.

Situation 2
Mr Smith bought a cordless drill set in a sale. The drill was reduced from £99·99 to £60·00. When Mr Smith got home, parts of the drill set were missing. Mr Smith complained to the store where he purchased the drill set, but they said that he did get it cheap and so they could do nothing about it.

Situation 3
Mr Smith wanted to buy a mobile phone to use on his trip to Italy. He told the salesman that this was the reason for buying the phone. When he got to Italy, the phone did not work. On return from his holiday he complained to the shop, who said that in order for the phone to work, he would have had to have bought a more expensive model.

Situation 4
Mr Smith bought a pair of trousers, described as waterproof, from a mail order catalogue. The first time he used them he got very wet.

Situation 5
Mr Smith went into the supermarket to buy some food. The cream cakes he was planning to buy were stored in a chiller cabinet which was recording a temperature of 10°C. He also bought some salmon labelled as 'Fresh Scottish Salmon' when in fact it was from a fish farm in Wales.

Situation 6
Mr Smith's local café has a caged bird in the food preparation area.

KU

Question 44

Study the label shown below.

(a)   (i)   List **five** items of information that must by law be found on this product label.
      (ii) Explain why **each** item of information might help the consumer when shopping.

(b)   (i)   List **three** items of information that do not, by law, have to be on this product label.
      (ii) Explain why **each** item of information might help the consumer when shopping.

KU **Question 45**

Diet can be a contributory factor in a range of diseases, including heart disease.

(a)   Other than diet, list **two** factors that can contribute to heart disease.

(b)   Explain how **each** factor contributes to this disease.

KU **Question 46**

Evaluate the suitability of the outfit below for a woman who is six months pregnant and who wishes to buy an outfit for the summer.

Smock:
- Made from 98% cotton and 2% elastane;
- Three-quarter length sleeves;
- V-neck;
- Slits on sleeve hem and sides;
- Available in the following colours: pink, green, white, yellow, striped or printed flower pattern;
- Sizes 6/8, 10/12, 14/16, 18/20, 22.

Trousers have:
- Adjustable elastic inside;
- Stretch mesh front panel;
- Button fastening;
- Inside leg – 74 cm;
- Sizes – 8, 10, 12, 14, 16, 18;
- Colours – cream, pink, green, yellow.

Management of expenditure

See pages 101–107 of Leckie & Leckie's *Standard Grade Home Economics Course Notes*.

KU **Question 47**

What is meant by the term 'balanced budget'?

KU **Question 48**

Mr and Mrs Jones are planning to buy a new dishwasher.

The model they are considering costs £299·99.

List the advantages and disadvantages of paying for the dishwasher by **each** of the following methods:

    (*a*)   cash;

    (*b*)   credit card;

    (*c*)   credit sale.

KU **Question 49**

A student has got into a situation where he has a large number of unpaid bills. The list of bills includes:

    •   student loan;

    •   credit card;

    •   rent;

    •   bank overdraft;

    •   store card.

What action should the student take in this situation?

Question 50

Read the information about Household A.

INFORMATION ABOUT THE MONTHLY INCOME AND EXPENDITURE OF HOUSEHOLD A

Income (net)	Amount
Salary (full-time)	£1300·00
Salary (part-time)	£300·00
Child benefit	£63·00

Expenditure	Amount
Food	£300·00
Clothing	£50·00
Mortgage	£400·00
Maintenance of house	£40·00
Electricity	£25·00
Gas	£25·00
Toiletries & household goods	£40·00
Insurance	£100·00
Council Tax	£105·00
Car running costs	£30·00
Road tax	£15·00
Car insurance	£10·00
TV Licence	£10·00
Loans/credit cards	£125·00
Telephone	£25·00
Mobile phone	£13·00
Savings	£10·00
Travelling expenses	£50·00
Club memberships	£65·00
Entertaining	£140·00
Holidays	£55·00
Nursery fees	£15·00
Birthdays and Christmas	£15·00
Total	**£1663·00**

Peter and Jane are a married couple in their early thirties.

They have one child, Jade, aged 2 years. Jane works two days a week, and the rest of the time she looks after Jade. Jane has recently been asked if she would like to work additional days, but she has refused as she likes to spend time with Jade. Peter works full-time and drives the 5-minute journey to work.

Jade goes to a private nursery one day a week and spends the other day at her grandparent's.

Answer the following questions about the household expenditure:

(a)   Which items of expenditure can be regarded as:

   (i)   fixed;
   (ii) variable.

(b)   Would you regard Household A's budget as a good budget or a poor budget? Explain your answer.

Peter has been made redundant. He has a new job to go to, but he does not start that job for another four months.

(c)   Devise a list of possible changes that the household will have to make to their budget over the next few months.

(d)   Explain **each** of the changes you have suggested.

Planning
and
carrying out
practical exercises

Throughout your Standard Grade course you will carry out a variety of practical exercises. These exercises are designed to assess your ability to:

- carry out a practical exercise making good use of the time available;
- carry out a practical exercise in an effective manner, whilst working safely and hygienically;
- demonstrate a variety of practical skills in a co-ordinated way.

One of the most important aspects of the practical exercise is planning. It is important to plan each practical exercise thoroughly. Planning will involve you in a variety of activities:

- choosing suitable items to make;
- preparing a food requisition/order sheet;
- preparing a time plan.

Let's look at each of these areas in turn and at the same time take you through an example of a practical exercise and how it should be planned.

Choosing suitable items to make

The first step of the exercise is to choose suitable items to make.

The following checklist outlines some of the areas you will have to think about before you select dishes to make.

You should use all the time you have available but you must complete the whole exercise within the given time-scale.

Remember that the more skills you demonstrate, the better your grade will be.

Areas to think about	Yes	No
Do the dishes show a range of practical skills?	✓	
Can you make the dishes in the given time-scale?	✓	
Have you read the recipes carefully to ensure that you can carry out all the processes involved?	✓	
Do you have all the resources and equipment required to make the recipes?	✓	

It is important that you read your recipes carefully to make sure that you understand the recipe instructions.

Some recipes require special preparation and cooking equipment.

Some recipes require special ingredients that may be difficult to obtain.

You may not be able to use some ingredients if they are expensive to buy.

TIP
If possible use a recipe that you have tried already, or adapt a recipe that you have tried already.

If the answer to any of the above questions is 'no' you will have to reconsider the dishes you have selected.

Here is an example of a possible practical exercise:

'Prepare a two-course meal for a vegetarian who chooses to eat dairy products and eggs.'

For this exercise you would have to consider the following:

- The meal has to be a two-course meal – starter and main course or main course and dessert.
- The meal must not contain any animal foods – although eggs, milk and cheese are acceptable.

The time allocated to this practical exercise is 80 minutes.

The following two dishes have been selected for the practical exercise:

- cheese and lentil bake;
- fruit salad flan.

The recipes are on pages 42 and 43.

When you have selected suitable items to make, your next step is to prepare a food requisition sheet.

Preparing a food requisition/order sheet

A food requisition/order sheet is really a shopping list. It details all the food, equipment and resources that you require to make a meal or dish. It contains not only a list of ingredients, but also the amounts required. You should always work in metric weights and measures.

In most cases you will be preparing food to serve two people. This may mean that you have to adjust quantities in a recipe when requisitioning.

Your teacher will provide you with a requisition sheet. It may not be the same as the one shown on page 44, but it will be similar. The requisition sheet has been prepared for the two dishes selected for the practical exercise. You will see that all items have been ordered under different categories.

Cheese and Lentil Bake

Ingredients

- 75g red lentils
- 250ml water
- $\frac{1}{2}$ onion
- 25g fresh bread
- 50g cheddar cheese
- 1·25ml spoon salt
- pinch of pepper
- $\frac{1}{2}$ egg
- 15ml lemon juice

Oven: Gas mark 5 / 190°C

Method

1. Set oven. Grease dish and place on baking tray.
2. Wash the lentils under the cold tap in a sieve.
3. Put the washed lentils in a pan with the water and simmer gently for about 15 minutes or until soft.
4. Peel and finely chop the onion and add it to the lentils as they are cooking.
5. Use the coarse side of a grater to make the breadcrumbs.
6. Grate the cheese. Beat the egg.
7. When the lentils are cooked, remove from the heat. Drain and stir in the cheese, breadcrumbs, salt, pepper and lemon juice.
8. Put the mixture into a greased ovenproof dish and bake for 30 minutes until golden brown.

Fruit Salad Flan

Ingredients

Pastry Ingredients:
- 50g plain flour
- 25g wholemeal flour
- 40g margarine
- 3 × 5ml spoons cold water

Filling Ingredients:
- $\frac{1}{2}$ red eating apple
- 1 × 15ml spoon lemon juice
- 50g cream cheese
- 25g black grapes
- 25g green grapes
- 1 small banana
- 1 × 15ml spoon lemon juice
- 25g drained mandarin orange segments

Topping Ingredients:
- 2 × 15ml spoons sieved apricot jam
- 1 × 15ml spoon lemon juice

Oven: Gas mark 6 / 200°C

Method

1. Set oven and collect a 15cm flan ring.
2. Measure the plain and wholemeal flour into a bowl; add margarine and rub until mixture resembles breadcrumbs.
3. Add enough water to make a stiff dough.
4. Knead lightly and roll out to fit the flan ring. Set aside for 5 minutes.
5. Bake pastry blind for 15–20 minutes until pastry is cooked. Cool.
6. Wash, peel, core and grate the half apple. Mix with 15ml of lemon juice and beat into the cream cheese.
7. Spread cream cheese onto the base of the cooled flan case.
8. Wash and halve the grapes. Remove any pips.
9. Peel and slice the banana and toss in 15ml of lemon juice.
10. Arrange the mandarin oranges, grapes and banana on the cheese mixture in the flan case.
11. Gently heat the apricot jam with 15ml of lemon juice. Beat well.
12. Brush apricot glaze over the fruit.
13. Serve.

Food Requisition Sheet

Name:	Christopher Ryan	Class:	S4 PQ
Teacher:	Mrs Cook	Date Required:	25th April

Items to be made: Cheese and Lentil Bake
Fruit Salad Flan

Meat and Fish	Quantity	Fruit and Vegetables	Quantity
		Onion	½
		Red apple	½
		Black grapes	25g
		Green grapes	25g
		Banana	1 small

Dairy Products	Quantity	Tins/Bottles/Dried	Quantity
Cheddar cheese	50g	Red lentils	75g
Margarine	40g	Salt	1·25ml
Cream cheese	50g	Lemon juice	60ml
		Plain flour	50g
		Wholemeal flour	25g
		Mandarin oranges	25g
		Apricot jam	30ml
		Pepper	pinch

Other Foods	Quantity	Equipment/Resources	
White bread (for breadcrumbs)	25g	Baking tray x 2	Grater
Eggs	½	Oil for greasing	Cook's Knife
		15cm flan ring	Vegetable Knife
		Food processor	
		Glazing brush	
		Baking beans	
		Greaseproof Paper	

Make sure this date is accurate, otherwise you will have no food to cook with!

All weights and measures are in metric.

The lemon juice is needed for both dishes.

It may seem odd to order half an egg, but there might be someone else in your class who could use the other half.

The food processor has been requisitioned, as it will be used to make the pastry.

It is normally neccessary to order items of equipment that are not stored in your work units.

Now that you have completed your food requisition sheet, you can prepare your time plan.

Preparing a time plan

The purpose of a time plan is to allow you to plan and time the sequence of activities that you will follow when carrying out the practical exercise.

The time plan below has been prepared for the vegetarian two-course meal. The time allocation for this practical exercise is 80 minutes.

Time Plan

Times	Activities	Notes
10·00–10·05	Wash hands, set oven and collect ingredients for the pastry.	
10·05–10·15	Make the pastry in the processor. Line flan ring with pastry. Leave to rest.	
10·15–10·20	Wipe table and clear away dishes. Collect ingredients for Cheese and Lentil Bake.	
10·20–10·25	Grease dish, put lentils on to cook for 15 mins. Place flan base in oven to cook.	Lentils ready – 10·40 Flan ready – 10·45
10·25–10·40	Prepare remaining ingredients for the dish.	
10·40–10·45	Drain lentils and complete the preparation of the Cheese and Lentil Bake. Place in oven (lower shelf).	Bake ready – 11·15
10·45–10·50	Remove flan case from oven and let it cool. Clear table and wash dishes.	
10·50–11·10	Prepare filling for the flan and assemble. Prepare topping for the flan.	
11·10–11·15	Glaze flan with topping. Remove Cheese and Lentil Bake.	
11·15–11·20	Serve both dishes. Final tidy.	

Times are normally allocated in a minimum of five-minute blocks.

It is important to plan time for tidying up and for washing dishes during the exercise.

The Lentil Bake is cooked at 190°C and the flan at 200°C. The Lentil Bake is placed on a lower shelf as this part of the oven will be cooler.

This column is useful for making notes such as oven temperatures and the finishing times of cooking processes.

Carrying out the practical exercise

So far you have done a lot of planning and preparation for the practical exercise. It is important that you put all this planning and preparation to good use before you actually carry out the practical exercise. Here are some tips that you should follow to ensure that all goes well on the day of your practical exercise assessment.

- Carefully double-check your requisition sheet and time plan before you hand them in to your teacher.

- Ask to see your time plan a few days before the assessment date and take the time plan and recipe sheets home with you. Read over the time plan and the recipe sheets several times.

- You should be able to work your way through the practical exercise without having to constantly read your recipe sheets.

- If possible try out your recipes and time plan in advance. If you need to change your time plan after this practice, do so – but remember to tell your teacher.

- If any of your recipes do not turn out as you expected, ask your teacher for some advice.

- Think about how you will serve the meal you make. Remember that the appearance of a meal is very important.

The
Practical
Assignment

The practical assignment involves you **analysing**, **planning**, **carrying out** and **evaluating** a practical activity. The practical activity will relate to an assignment brief, which will be issued to you by your teacher. You will complete this work on a pro forma issued by the Scottish Qualifications Authority (SQA).

You will be allocated a maximum of 360 minutes to complete the practical assignment. At least 100 minutes should be allocated to carrying out practical work, leaving up to 260 minutes for the analysing, planning and evaluation.

The assignment brief is the starting point. This outlines what you will have to do. Here is an example of an assignment brief:

'Provide seasonal gift(s) for the local residential home.'

You can see from the assignment brief that you will have to make an item or items – in this case seasonal gifts.

An assignment brief will require you to make either food or textile items – or a combination of both. What is important is that the items that you decide to make are suitable for the situation given in the assignment brief. This is where your **analysing** and **planning** becomes important.

Your starting point is to complete the front page of the pro forma provided by SQA. It will look something like the pro forma opposite. Remember that you are allocating times to what you **plan** to do.

Your teacher will give you the start and finish dates. In total, the assignment will take no more than 360 minutes.

Start date: November 12th   **Finish date:** December 2nd

Complete the clear parts of the chart below to give a brief outline plan for your practical assignment.

The shaded areas are to be completed by your teacher.

Activity	Dates	Time Allocation	Grade	Teacher comments to justify grades
Analysing	November 12th	60 minutes		
Planning	November 19th	60 minutes		
Carrying out	November 26th December 1st	120 minutes		
Evaluating	December 2nd	60 minutes		
Overall Grade				

The total amount of time allocated to carrying out must be at least 100 minutes.

The grey areas are for your teacher only. You must not write in these parts.

Analysing the assignment

When you are analysing the assignment you should be thinking to yourself:

'If I had to do this for real what are all the important things that I will have to consider before I can decide on what to make?'

There will be clues in the wording of the assignment brief to help you.

The first stage of analysing is to identify all the key points of the assignment brief. This is easy to do as you only need to underline the important words in the assignment brief. This has been done below:

'Provide seasonal gift(s) for the local residential home.'

This assignment brief has five key points. The assignment brief will **never** have more than eight key points.

There may however be other things that you would need to consider before selecting items to make for the assignment. One example might be cost. This word is not in the assignment brief, but it is important. This is known as an **additional point**. The **maximum** number of additional points that you should identify is **four**.

Once you have identified the key and additional points, you then have to explain why you have to consider each of the points. The more detail you can provide, the better the grade you will get.

Look at the example provided below:

	Key Point	Explanation of how the key point links to the assignment brief
1	Provide	I will have to provide the gifts to the home and so I must be able to make whatever I choose.
2	Seasonal	The dates that I have been given for the assignment mean that it will be finished in December, so it should have a Christmas/winter theme.
3	Gift(s)	I have to give a food or textile item to an elderly person in the home, so I would need to take into account their needs before choosing items.

The underlined key points have been written into the correct part of the pro forma and an explanation has been given as to why this point is important.

You should do this for **all** the key and additional points that you have identified.

Having identified all the key and additional points and explained why they are important for this assignment you can now start to think about possible items to make. This is called the planning strand.

Planning the assignment

You will need to look through lots of recipe books, textile patterns and other resources to decide on suitable items to make. Remember, whatever you decide to make they should meet all the key and additional points that you have identified earlier – i.e. **each** product you select to make **must** meet **all** the key and additional points.

Remember that you have only got **360 minutes in total** to analyse, plan, carry out and evaluate the practical assignment. When you have decided on suitable items to make, you need to give reasons why you have selected each item.

Let's say that you were thinking about shortbread and strawberry tarts as gifts, you would need to complete the next part of the pro forma.

List your key points here.

List your additional points here.

Use the chart below to list the items that you could make and tick which **key points** and **additional points** are met.

List the items that you could make here	List your key points here	Provide	Seasonal	Gifts	Local	Residential home				List your additional points here	Cost			
		1	2	3	4	5	6	7	8		9	10	11	12
		Use a tick (✓) if the item meets the key point or additional point.												
Shortbread		✓	✓	✓	✓	✓					✓			
Strawberry tarts		✓	✗	✓	✓	✓					✗			

This is not seasonal or inexpensive and so is not suitable.

If the item **does not** meet the requirement, either put in a cross or do not tick the box.

Do this for all the products that you think you could make. If the product meets the requirement, insert a ✓.

The next stage is to decide what items you will make to meet the needs of the assignment.

Look at the pro forma below:

Use the box below to list the items you have chosen to make.	
1 Shortbread	4
2	5
3	6

You should only select items that have been given ticks for all the key and additional points.

If you select items that do not have ticks, this means that the item does not meet all the needs of the brief.

You can only make a maximum of six items.

Remember when choosing items, you must spend a minimum of 100 minutes making the items.

This means that for food-based assignments you will probably be making at least **two** items. For textile assignments you will probably make only **one** item.

The next part of the planning strand involves explaining why you have decided to make each of the items you have selected. You must do this for all the items you have selected, and you must link your explanations for choice to each of the key points and additional points.

Look at the example below. This shows you the explanations for the choice of shortbread for all the key and additional points.

Use the following chart:
- **Explain** why you have chosen **each** item that you will make.
- Your explanation **must** link back to **each** of the **key points** and **additional points** you identified.

Item to be made	Key Point No.	Explanation (Linked to each of the key points and additional points – bullet points should be used.)
Shortbread	1	• I will be making shortbread using my own skills and so will be meeting the requirement of providing.
	1, 2	• Shortbread can be classed as a seasonal gift as it is traditional to have this type of product at Christmas and New Year and I will be giving this as a Christmas gift to an elderly person.
	2, 3	• The product is a food product which will be carefully packaged and wrapped to become a Christmas gift.
	4	• The residential home is local and so transporting the product to the home will not be a problem.
	5	• The residential home is for elderly people living on their own. They can eat the shortbread with tea or coffee and there will be enough to share with friends.
	9	• The cost to make the shortbread will be minimal as I am using only basic store cupboard ingredients.

Remember to explain your choice for each item selected.

Remember your explanations should cover each key and additional point.

You may be able to explain more than one key or additional point within one explanation.

Your explanations should be bullet-pointed.

Planning for the practical activities

Before making the item or items you have selected you will need to ensure that you have:

1. Completed a requisition sheet for all the resources and equipment that you need;

2. It is also a good idea to develop a work sequence. The work sequence should include:

   - the date that you plan to do the work;

   - how long you have to do the work;

   - the sequence of activities that you will do in this time.

Here is an example:

Work Sequence		Comments (As you work, use this column to record any good points or problems you meet or changes you make.)
November 26th 60 minutes	Make shortbread. Cool and store.	The oven was faulty and this meant I had to reheat another oven. However I managed to finish on time.

A work sequence is not the same as a time plan. A time plan gives much more detail. You do not have to develop a time plan for this part of the assignment.

Remember your work sequence is not marked. However, it will ensure that you have all the items made in time.

It is also an idea to make a note of things that went well during the making of the item(s), as well as things that do not go to plan, or which did not work out.

The comments will be useful to you when you come to do your evaluation. It can be easy to forget things when you come to write your evaluation and so spending a short time at the end of each practical lesson writing a few notes is worthwhile.

You are now ready to move onto the carrying out strand of the assignment.

Carrying out the assignment

This is where you will be making the items that you have selected, following your sequence of work. You will be assessed by your teacher/lecturer whilst doing this work. You will be assessed on your ability to:

- follow instructions;
- make efficient use of equipment, time and materials;
- follow hygiene and safety procedures.

It is important that you try to do your best when completing the practical work. If possible ,try to make your items in advance. If any of your items do not turn out as you expected, ask your teacher for some advice.

When you have made all your items you are ready for the last part of the practical assignment – the evaluation.

Evaluating the assignment

The evaluating strand is divided into three sections. Each section will take you through the process of evaluating the product (the items that you have made) and the process (carrying out the practical assignment).

Let's look at each section in turn, continuing to use the shortbread as our example.

The first section of the evaluating strand asks you to evaluate the items you have made using a simple sensory evaluation chart.

Look at the example below:

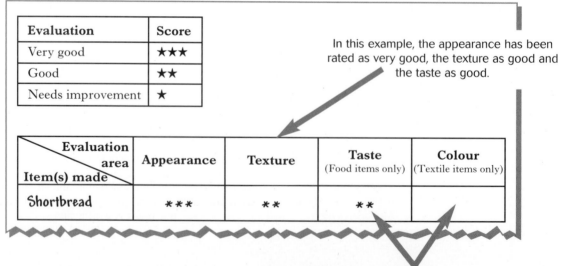

Evaluation	Score
Very good	★★★
Good	★★
Needs improvement	★

In this example, the appearance has been rated as very good, the texture as good and the taste as good.

Evaluation area / Item(s) made	Appearance	Texture	Taste (Food items only)	Colour (Textile items only)
Shortbread	✷✷✷	✷✷	✷✷	

For both food and textile items you complete the evaluation for appearance and texture. You would then complete the taste box for food items **only** and the colour box for textile items **only**.

You do this for **each** item that you have made.

In the next section of the evaluating strand, you have to justify the rating that you have given to each item for appearance, texture and taste or colour.

If you are working at Credit level you can miss out this section and move onto the next evaluation section.

Look at the example below:

Item(s) made	Score given	Explanation for the score given for appearance.
Shortbread	✱ ✱ ✱	• The end product was golden brown and glistened with the sugar that was sprinkled on top. • The colour was straw brown and the shortbread mould that I used gave a nice thistle pattern on top of the shortbread.

Item(s) made	Score given	Explanation for the score given for texture.
Shortbread	✱ ✱	• The texture was good, but perhaps the shortbread was slightly too thick as the inside of the shortbread was slightly chewy. • I could perhaps have made one large and some small shortbreads instead of making one thicker one.

Item(s) made	Score given	Explanation for the score given for taste.
Shortbread	✱ ✱	• The shortbread had a nice sweet taste, but because I used margarine and not butter, it did not taste as nice as some butter shortbread that I have tasted before.

Remember that when giving an explanation for the rating, try to explain why the product was only given a 'good' texture rating and not a 'very good' texture rating.

If the product needed some improvement, try to say why and what the improvement would be.

Remember, you do this for **each** product and for **each** rating area.

In this section, the comments made for each area of appearance, texture and taste link back to the ratings given earlier.

You have now evaluated each of the products that you have made. It is now time to evaluate how well you have worked your way through the practical assignment.

In this last section of the evaluation, you are asked to make an evaluative comment on how well you carried out the analysing, planning and carrying out strands of the practical assignment, as well as commenting on the end products.

It might be useful to make notes for yourself as you work through each strand. You can refer to these when you are completing the evaluating section.

Look at the example below:

When evaluating how well you did in each strand, your comments should link to either:

- skills/abilities;
- time;
- resources.

Evaluative comment on analysing.

- I think I carried out the analysing section well as I identified five key points and one additional point. I could not think of any more additional points, and cost was an important additional point as I had a very limited budget to work to.

Evaluative comment on planning.

- In my planning I had identified six products to make. This was probably one product too many as I was very rushed to get everything made. If I was to do this again I would take more care when planning my practical lessons to make sure all could be done in the time available.

Evaluative comment on carrying out.

- When I went to make the shortbread, the oven did not work and so I had to change ovens. This took up some time, but I did manage to make the shortbread on time and to a good standard.

Evaluative comment on final items.

- All of my final items were edible, although the shortbread was a little chewy in the centre. Given that they were all edible – and my friends certainly ate them all – I think that all my products were reasonably successful and met the requirements of the assignment.

Remember that in this section your comments must be evaluative. This means that you must back up every statement that you make with an explanation.

If there are things that you could have done better, state this in your evaluation and say how it might have improved the assignment.

For Credit level you should give a minimum of one evaluative comment for each of the four areas.

Remember evaluating is not just talking about all the things that went badly. If something went well, then say that and explain why it went well.

Pull out answer section for Leckie & Leckie's
Questions in Standard Grade Home Economics

Note, in the answer section the use of the '/' means that this is an alternative answer. For example: 'The use of this book can help you with the examination/help to answer the questions in this book.'

Eating a variety of foods contributes to health

Question 1

(a) and (b)

When answering this question, make sure that your answers relate back to an eight-year-old child.

Main* nutrients found in contents of the pack lunch box			
Orange	Semi-skimmed milk	Wholemeal bread	Chocolate (on raisins)
• Vitamin C • Carbohydrate • Vitamin A	• Protein • Fat • Vitamin D • Calcium • Phosphorus • Vitamin B (B1 and B2) • Vitamin K	• Protein • Carbohydrate • Vitamin B (B1 and B2) • Fat • Sodium • Folic Acid • Iron • Phosphorus • Vitamin E	• Protein • Carbohydrate • Fat • Iron • Calcium • Vitamin B (B1 and B2)

Main* nutrients found in contents of the pack lunch box (cont.)			
Tomato	Cucumber	Chicken	Raisins
• Vitamin C	• Vitamin C	• Protein • Fat	• Carbohydrate • Iron

* Some of the food sources listed above may contain other nutrients in small amounts, but are not considered main food sources.

---

1. (c)   Protein

- Required for growth and repair of body tissues. Useful because a child of this age will be growing rapidly.

- Excess protein can be used as a source of energy and this may be useful to an eight-year-old child as they tend to be active.

Carbohydrate

- A major source of energy that will be useful to an eight-year-old child as they tend to be active.

- Excess carbohydrate may be stored as fat in the body so can provide warmth, which may be necessary as a young child will lose more heat than an adult.

Fat

- A major source of energy that will be useful to an eight-year-old child as they tend to be active.

- Excess fat may be stored as fat in the body so can provide warmth, which may be necessary as a young child will lose more heat than an adult.

- Provides fat soluble nutrients that are essential to the correct development of an eight-year-old child.

- This is a period of rapid growth and development for an eight-year-old child who will require an adequate source of fat soluble vitamins which can be found in fat.

- Provides essential fatty acids which have an important role to play in the correct development of an eight-year-old child.

1. (c) cont.

Vitamin A
- Required for the correct rate of growth and development in children and so a good supply is needed.
- Assists with the development of good vision – particularly night vision – and as the eight-year-old child is still developing, a good supply is required.
- Required to protect the surface tissues – e.g. of the nose and mouth. As the child will still be developing and growing such tissues at this stage a good supply is required.

Vitamin D
- This is a time of rapid growth and development for this age group and a good supply of Vitamin D is required to ensure the development of strong bones and teeth.
- Assists in the healing of broken bones – active children may break bones at this age.

Vitamin E
- This vitamin is associated with the formation of cell membranes and, at this stage of rapid growth and development, a good supply is necessary.
- This is an anti-oxidant vitamin and will assist in the longer term prevention of certain types of cancer.

Vitamin K
- This age group is active and may be prone to accidents. Vitamin K will assist in the clotting of blood when there are cuts or grazes after falls.

Vitamin C
- This vitamin is associated with the formation of connective tissue and, at this stage of rapid growth and development, a good supply is necessary.
- This nutrient is required to ensure the good absorption of iron. This age group is active and so iron is needed to carry oxygen to all the body tissues.
- Children of this age can pick up infections from other children and so a good supply of Vitamin C will assist in the prevention of infection.
- This vitamin is associated with the formation of the walls of blood vessels and at this stage of rapid growth and development, a good supply is necessary.

Vitamin B1
- This vitamin assists in the release of energy from carbohydrates and, as this age group may be active, energy requirement may be high.
- This is a time of rapid growth and development for this age group and a good supply of Vitamin B1 is required to ensure the growth and functioning of the nervous system.
- At this age, muscles will be developing and growing so Vitamin B1 is required to ensure correct muscle tone.
- This age group may be active and thus be using a wide range of different muscles; Vitamin B1 is required to ensure that muscles remain toned.

Vitamin B2
- This vitamin assists in the release of energy from carbohydrates, proteins and fats and as this age group may be active, energy requirement may be high.
- Required for the correct rate of growth and development in children and so a good supply is required.

Folic acid
- At this stage of development, a good supply of folic acid is required to ensure that red blood cells form correctly.
- Red blood cells carry oxygen to the body tissues. As children in this age group may be active, a good supply of oxygen to tissues is required. This can be assisted by a good supply of folic acid.

Iron
- Required for red blood cell development and this is crucial at this stage of development for an eight-year-old when blood capacity increases with body growth.
- Red blood cells carry oxygen to the body tissues. As children in this age group may be active, a good supply of oxygen to tissues is required. This will be assisted by a good supply of iron.

Calcium
- This is a time of growth and development for this age group and so plenty of calcium is required for developing bones and teeth.
- This age group is active and may be prone to accidents. Calcium will assist in the clotting of blood when there are cuts or grazes after falls.
- This is a time of rapid growth and development for this age group and a good supply of calcium is required to ensure the functioning of the nervous system/nerves.
- At this age muscles will be developing and growing so calcium is required to ensure correct muscle function.
- This age group may be active and thus be using a wide range of different muscles, calcium is required to ensure muscles function correctly.

Sodium
- Required to maintain the correct concentration of body fluids which can at this stage of development be crucial to future health.
- This is a time of rapid growth and development for this age group and a supply of sodium is required to ensure the functioning of the nervous system/nerves.
- At this age, muscles will be developing and growing so sodium is required to ensure correct muscle function.
- This age group may be active and thus be using a wide range of different muscles, sodium is required to ensure muscles function correctly.

Phosphorus
- Works with calcium to ensure the correct growth and development of bones and teeth for this age group.
- This age group is active and may be prone to accidents. Phosphorus will act with calcium to assist in the clotting of blood when there are cuts or grazes after falls.
- Has a role to play in obtaining energy from foods and this is important for children of this age group because they are active and so require a ready source of energy.

Question 2

(a)
- Vitamin A
- Vitamin C
- Vitamin E

(b)
- May help reduce the incidence of cancer and heart disease in later life.
- Vitamin C protects against certain cancer types in later life.
- Vitamins A and C can lower the risk of heart disease in later life.

Question 3

(a) Any two from:
- We cannot survive without a regular intake of water and so it is essential to life.
- A regular intake of water can prevent dehydration.
- Without the appropriate balance of water, correct bodily functions cannot take place – e.g. regulation of temperature through sweating, disposal of waste products through urine.
- Allows for the absorption of nutrients in the body and so assists in general health.

- A lack of water can lead to possible malfunction of internal organs.

(b) Any two from:
- Assists in the production of soft faeces which allow waste products to be excreted from the body easily. This prevents diseases such as constipation and haemorrhoids (piles).
- Assists in the production of soft faeces which means that waste products can travel through the digestive system. This prevents diseases such as diverticular disease and bowel cancer.
- Can assist in the removal of potentially dangerous toxins from the body and so assist in health promotion.
- Provides a feeling of fullness and so may assist in the prevention of snacking which can lead to obesity.
- May help in the prevention of coronary heart disease as it is thought that NSP can assist in the removal of cholesterol from the body.

Question 4

Liver and orange juice
- Liver is a good source of iron. Orange juice is a good source of Vitamin C.
- Vitamin C assists in the absorption of iron in the body by converting it to a form that is readily absorbed.
- This combination will assist with iron absorption.

Milk and cheese
- Milk is a good source of protein, calcium, phosphorous and Vitamin D and contains lactose. Cheese is a good source of protein, calcium, Vitamin D and phosphorous.
- Calcium and phosphorous work together to produce calcium phosphate which hardens the bones and teeth.
- Vitamin D regulates the amount of calcium absorbed by the body and so a lack of Vitamin D has a knock-on effect on the amount of calcium absorbed by the body.
- Lactose, which is the sugar found in milk, can assist the absorption of calcium by the body.
- This combination will assist with calcium absorption.

Spinach and milk
- Milk is a good source of calcium. Spinach contains a type of acid called oxalic acid which prevents the absorption of calcium.
- This combination may reduce/inhibit calcium absorption.

Question 5

(a)

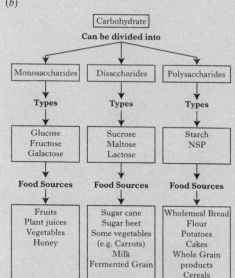

Protein

Can be divided into

| Low biological value | High biological value |

Food Sources

Food Sources

| Beans
Peas
Nuts
Lentils
Cereals | Eggs
Milk
Cheese
Meat
Fish
Soya bean |

(b)

Carbohydrate

Can be divided into

| Monosaccharides | Disaccharides | Polysaccharides |

Types — **Types** — **Types**

| Glucose
Fructose
Galactose | Sucrose
Maltose
Lactose | Starch
NSP |

Food Sources — **Food Sources** — **Food Sources**

| Fruits
Plant juices
Vegetables
Honey | Sugar cane
Sugar beet
Some vegetables
(e.g. Carrots)
Milk
Fermented Grain | Wholemeal Bread
Flour
Potatoes
Cakes
Whole Grain
products
Cereals |

(c)

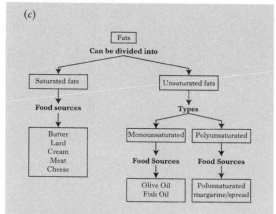

Fats

Can be divided into

| Saturated fats | Unsaturated fats |

Food sources — **Types**

| Butter
Lard
Cream
Meat
Cheese | | Monounsaturated | Polyunsaturated |

Food Sources — **Food Sources**

| Olive Oil
Fish Oil | Polunsaturated
margarine/spread |

Question 6

(a)   Chocolate Drink.

(b)   MaltoChoc 'Light' Drink.

(c)   Malted Chocolate Drink.

(d)   The MaltoChoc 'Light' drink has almost
       the same kJ content as the MaltoChoc
       drink and has a much higher fat content.
       This is despite it being sold as a 'light'
       product.

(e)   Any one of:

- source of energy;

- source of warmth/heat;

- provides essential fatty acids;

- source of fat soluble vitamins.

Current dietary advice

Question 7

(a) and (b)

Any six from:

Fruit and vegetables

- advised to eat more;

- intake to double;

- intake to double to 400 g per day.

Carrot and coriander soup contributes to
the vegetable part of this target.

Fresh fruit kebab contributes to the fruit
part of this target.

Bread

- advised to eat more;

- intake to increase, mainly using
  wholemeal bread;

- intake to increase by 45% from present
  daily intake.

The homemade bread contributes to this
target.

Total Complex Carbohydrates (TCC)
- advised to eat more;
- intake to increase by a quarter through fruit, vegetables, bread, breakfast cereals, rice, pasta and potatoes;
- intake to increase by 25% through fruit, vegetables, bread, breakfast cereals, rice, pasta. Potato intake to increase by 25%.

The soup has vegetables and so assists with this target.

Bread is a source of TCC and so contributes to this target.

Pasta is a TCC and so contributes to this target.

The fruit will contain TCCs and so contribute to this target.

Fish
- advised to eat more fish, especially oily fish;
- intake of oily fish to double;
- intake of oily fish to double from 44g per week to 88g per week.

Tuna is an oily fish and so meets with the specific target to increase consumption of oily fish.

Salt
- advised to eat less salt;
- average intake to reduce;
- average intake to reduce from 163 mmol per day to 100 mmol per day.

The use of coriander in the soup may mean that less salt is needed and so assists with this target.

There are no other obvious salt sources in this meal unless added to the pasta/bread and so this would contribute overall to the salt reduction target.

Fat
- advised to eat less fat, especially saturated fat;
- average intake of total fat to be reduced;
- average intake of saturated fat to be reduced;
- average intake of total fat to be reduced to no more than 35% of food energy;
- average intake of saturated fat to be reduced to no more than 11% of food energy.

The cooking methods here do not add fat to the meal and so assist with the total fat reduction target.

Low fat yoghurt will contribute to the total fat reduction target.

The tuna is a source of unsaturated fat and so this will assist in the overall reduction of saturated fat in the diet.

Sugar
- adults not to increase intake;
- intake by children to reduce by half;
- adult intake of non-milk extrinsic (NME) sugars not to rise;
- intake of NME sugars by children to reduce by half;
- intake of NME sugars by children to reduce to less than 10% of energy.

There are no obvious sources of sugar in this menu, so contributing to the target to reduce/not increase sugar intake.

The fruit will be a source of natural/intrinsic sugar and so is a good choice of dessert which links with the targets not to increase/to reduce sugar intake.

Question 8

(a) and (b)

Any five from:

Cream of tomato soup

Change by not adding cream to the soup.

Reason: The cream is rich in saturated fat which can contribute to coronary heart disease.

The cream adds fat to the menu and removing it will reduce fat content.

White bread roll

Change to a wholemeal bread roll.

Reason: The wholemeal bread roll will assist with the target to increase bread consumption using mainly wholemeal bread.

The bread roll will contribute to the target to increase the total complex carbohydrate content of the diet.

Deep fried battered salmon

Change the cooking method to steaming/baking/grilling/poaching/microwaving.

Reason: Deep frying adds fat to the menu and so changing to a fat free method of cooking will assist with the fat reduction target.

Note: if steaming, grilling, poaching or microwaving, the batter would not be used.

8. cont.

Garlic mayonnaise dip

Change dip to garlic dip made with low fat mayonnaise/low fat yoghurt/fromage frais/no dip.

Reason: Mayonnaise contains a large amount of fat and low/reduced fat versions will reduce the fat content of the meal.

Serving the salmon with no dip will eliminate fat from that part of the menu.

Serving the salmon with an alternative low fat dip will reduce fat from that part of the menu.

Baked potato with butter

Remove the butter/change to polyunsaturated fat/low fat spread.

Reason: Butter is a high fat food and so can be removed from the meal to help with the fat target.

Butter is a source of saturated fat in the diet and removal of butter from the potato will assist with the target to reduce saturated fat content.

Although polyunsaturated fat contains as much fat as butter, the fat is polyunsaturated and so less harmful to the body. This will assist in the reduction of saturated fat in the diet, but not total fat.

Low fat spread could be substituted as it has a lower fat content so contributing to the reduction of fat in the diet.

Low fat spreads tend to be based on either poly or mono unsaturated fats and so assists in the reduction of saturated fat.

Fresh fruit salad in light syrup

Change by removing light syrup/serving in natural fruit juice instead.

Reason: Light syrup will contain sugar and removal of the syrup will assist with the target to cut sugar intake.

Serving in natural juice will reduce the amount of sugar in the meal and so assist with the sugar reduction target.

If natural fruit juice is used in place of the syrup, this will contribute to the target to increase fruit and vegetable intake.

Ice cream

Change by serving with low fat ice cream/low fat yoghurt/fromage frais.

Reason: Ice cream has a high fat content and so replacing it with a low fat version will assist in reducing total fat content.

Some types of ice cream can have a high saturated fat content and replacing with a low fat version will help with the target to reduce saturated fat content.

Replacing ice cream with a low fat alternative (e.g. low fat yoghurt/fromage frais) will assist in the reduction of the total fat content of the meal.

Question 9

(a) Steaming

- No fat is added during this cooking process and so assists with the target to reduce total fat content.

- The food does not come into direct contact with water and so nutritional loss of vitamins is limited.

(b) Stir frying

- Only a minimal amount of fat is added during this process and so fat content is only increased slightly.

- Because this is a quick method of cooking, loss of vitamins and minerals is minimal.

(c) Microwave cooking

- No fat is added during this cooking process and so assists with the target to reduce total fat content.

- Only a limited amount of water needs to be added and so vitamin loss through leaching is reduced.

- Because this is a quick method of cooking, loss of vitamins and minerals is minimal.

Question 10

(a) Excess of fat

- Excess fat can lead to a person being overweight.

- Excessive amounts of fat can lead to obesity.
- Where the diet is high in saturated fats, the cholesterol level of the blood can increase. High levels of blood cholesterol can lead to coronary heart disease.
- Being overweight can place strain on the bones as additional weight is being carried.
- Being overweight can place additional strain on internal organs if excessive fat is surrounding the organs.

(b) Lack of NSP
- Lack of NSP can lead to constipation as the faeces become hard and difficult to move through the digestive tract.
- If a person has constipation, the effort required to pass waste products is increased and this can lead to haemorrhoids.
- Where waste products are sitting in the intestines for a long period of time, cells may become pre-cancerous/cancerous, causing bowel cancer/intestinal cancer later in life.
- NSP can assist in the removal of toxins and cholesterol from the body so if it is lacking, there is more chance of damage to health.
- May lead to diverticular disease as the faeces become hard and difficult to move round the intestinal tract.

(c) Lack of folic acid
- A lack of folic acid can lead to problems with foetal development (early stages of pregnancy) and the foetus can become deformed.
- Commonly associated with spina bifida.
- Can lead to a special form of anaemia.

Question 11

(a) (i) Bread Type D
    (ii) • This has the highest NSP content per slice and so would be good for a person wishing to follow a healthy eating programme.
    - Has the equal lowest salt content per slice of all the breads and so contributes to Sandy's attempt to follow healthy eating advice to reduce salt consumption.
    - Has the lowest fat content per slice and so contributes to Sandy's attempt to follow healthy eating advice to reduce total fat consumption.

- Has no added fat and so contributes to Sandy's attempt to follow healthy eating advice to reduce total fat consumption.
- Has no added sugar and so contributes to Sandy's attempt to follow healthy eating advice to reduce sugar consumption.

(b) C

(c) B

(d) A

(e) • Bread C has added folic acid. A good supply of folic acid is advised for both partners when planning for pregnancy.
- Bread B has added germ which is a good source of iron. If a person is anaemic he/she should be increasing consumption of foods containing iron.
- Bread A is made with organic flour. This means that care has been taken during the production of the flour to ensure the environment has not been harmed – e.g. via chemical spraying.

(f) The symbol of the Soil Association.

Question 12
- The load up plan is a plan designed to cover two main meals and a snack, whereas the late night takeaway is designed only for one meal and so the load up plan is a better health choice.
- The load up plan has slightly less calories covering two meals and a snack than the late night takeaway and so is a better health choice.
- The load up plan has less fat covering two meals and a snack than the late night takeaway and so is a better health choice.
- The late night meal is taken at a time when the body will soon be going into a resting phase and so very little energy will be burned. This makes this meal less suitable than the load up plan.
- The load up plan has a wider range of foods and nutrients and so makes it a healthier plan.
- The load up plan also has a wide range of food products that would contribute to meeting healthy eating targets.

Individuals have varying dietary needs

Question 13

Remember that in this question your answers must link back to an overweight 12-year-old male.

Energy

- The energy intake from the meal is very high compared to the EAR and for an overweight boy so may mean that the excess energy is stored as fat.
- Although 12-year-old boys may be active and so may require a good source of energy, it is unlikely that the overweight boy is active and so the excess will probably be stored as fat.

Protein

- The protein intake for the boy is very high compared to the RNI, but it does mean that he will have sufficient protein for growth and repair of body tissues and this is a time of growth for a 12-year-old.
- Excess protein – and there is excess in this diet – may be converted into fat and stored in the body – so adding to the overweight problem for this boy.
- Excess protein can be used as a source of energy should the body require it, but given that the diet is already high in energy any excess will be converted to fat and so add to the overweight problem.

Iron

- The iron intake is lower than the RNI and as the body capacity of a 12-year-old will be increasing, and so the blood volume increasing, iron is required to ensure the development of red blood cells.
- The lack of iron may mean that the boy suffers from anaemia and so becomes tired and inactive and less likely to take part in exercise which would burn off extra energy from the meal.
- Iron is required to develop a substance in the blood that helps to carry oxygen to body tissues. If it is lacking the boy may become tired and listless, not exercise and so add to the overweight problem.

Calcium

- The calcium content is almost correct. A teenage boy needs calcium for strong bones and teeth and this diet will provide the correct amount of calcium.
- An overweight boy's bones will have to carry excess weight and so it is important that the correct amount of calcium is being consumed.

- Whether all the calcium can be utilised for strong bones and teeth is dependent on having the correct amount of Vitamin D and phosphorus in the diet. We cannot tell this from this diet.
- Boys at this age may have accidents and thus bleed. Calcium assists with the clotting of blood and as this diet has the correct amount this should not be a problem.
- Calcium is required for the correct functioning of muscles and a 12-year-old boy will still have developing muscles. This diet provides the correct amount of calcium for this function.
- Calcium is required for the correct functioning of nerves as a 12-year-old boy will still have a developing nervous system. Therefore, a good source of calcium is required. This diet provides the correct amount of calcium for this function.

Vitamin C

- The vitamin C content is lower than the RNI. Vitamin C is required for the formation of connective tissues and as the 12-year-old is growing a good supply of vitamin C is vital.
- Vitamin C assists with the absorption of iron. Given that iron is short in the diet, it is important that as much iron is absorbed as possible. The low intake of vitamin C will not assist this process and the boy may suffer anaemia.
- Vitamin C helps to prevent infections, and 12-year-old school children may pick these up readily. There is more chance of this happening as the vitamin C intake is low.
- Vitamin C is essential for the formation of blood vessel walls. As the 12-year-old will be growing this process is important. If there is insufficient vitamin C in the diet and if this pattern continues the child's development may be affected.

Sodium

- The sodium content of the meal is excessive. Excess sodium has links to hypertension as does being overweight, so this boy is at increased risk of hypertension.
- Excessive sodium intake can harm internal organs if they are developing. The internal organs of a 12-year-old boy will still be developing and so he may come to harm later in life.
- Sodium is required for the correct functioning of muscles and, as a 12-year-old boy will still have developing muscles, this diet provides sufficient sodium to cover this function.
- Sodium is required for the correct functioning of nerves and, as a 12-year-old boy will still have a developing nervous system, a good source of salt is required. This diet provides sufficient sodium for this function.

Question 14

(a) Lacto vegetarian – foods A, B, G

Vegan – foods A, B, C, D, G, I

Pregnant woman – foods A, D

Note:
Some cheeses are made using a substance extracted from the stomach of calves and so would not be suitable for lacto vegetarians.

Some crisps contain a sugar derived from milk, which would make them unsuitable for vegans.

(b) Lacto vegetarians do not eat foods that directly result from the death of an animal or which are associated with animal death and so these foods are excluded.

Vegans eat no animal products and all these products are from animals. Chocolate contains milk.

Pregnant women should not eat soft cheeses as they may contain listeria bacteria which can cause foetal damage. Pregnant women should not eat foods rich in vitamin A, as this can be toxic. Liver is rich in vitamin A.

Question 15

Vegans may find it difficult to gain sufficient food sources of vitamin D, as it is not readily found in plants. However, the action of sunlight on a pigment in our skin can cause the body to make its own supply of vitamin D. This would prevent any deficiency from occurring.

Question 16

Remember that in this question your answers must link back to a 66-year-old female.

Energy
- The energy intake is double what it should be. As people age they may become less active and so their energy needs are reduced. This lady is at risk of becoming overweight if this pattern continues.
- This excess energy will be stored as fat in the body and so the lady may become overweight/obese.

Protein
- The protein intake is less than that recommended. This is not good for this lady as a daily intake of protein is required for the maintenance of body tissues.
- The lady is elderly and so there is more chance of protein being required to repair body tissues. This is less likely to happen if the protein intake is continually low.
- The body has a need for protein, and if it cannot be found from food sources, it can replenish supplies from muscles. This leads to muscle wastage and will not help with the long term health of an elderly person.

Vitamin B1
- The vitamin B1 content of the meal is slightly over that suggested by the RNI, but this is not a problem as the excess will be removed by the body.
- The amount of vitamin B1 being consumed is sufficient to ensure that its functions are carried out:
- Releasing energy from carbohydrates so that the elderly person will have sufficient energy sources to meet her needs.
- For maintenance of the nervous system to ensure the elderly person's nerves function correctly.
- Ensure that muscles remain as toned as possible – important for this person who has a protein deficiency/for an elderly person who may not be as mobile as she used to be and so muscles are exercised less.

Calcium
- The calcium intake is less than that required. This is not an ideal situation as calcium is required to maintain bone and teeth strength/density.
- Elderly women can be prone to less strong bones/osteoporosis and to falls. If the calcium content of the diet is low, there is more chance of bone breakage resulting from a fall.
- Calcium is also required for the clotting of blood. If an elderly person cuts themselves, then blood loss may be greater than it needs to be.
- Calcium is linked to muscle tone. This is important for this person who may not be as mobile as she used to be and so her muscles may be exercised less.

Vitamin D
- The vitamin D content is lower than that required. This is not ideal as vitamin D works with calcium to promote strong bones and teeth. If both the calcium and vitamin D content of the diet are low, there is less chance of strong bones and teeth.
- Vitamin D controls the amount of calcium absorbed by the body. If this is deficient then the amount of calcium that is absorbed (and this is deficient) will be reduced. This means that both bones and teeth may become weak.
- Elderly women can be prone to less strong bones/osteoporosis and to falls. If the vitamin D content of the diet is low, there is more chance of bone breakage resulting from a fall.
- Vitamin D promotes the healing of broken bones. If the elderly person has a broken bone, then the healing process will be slowed.

16. cont.

NSP

- The amount of NSP in the diet is less than that required. This will not help the lady with her constipation problem.

- Calcium absorption is hindered by NSP. However this is not a good reason to have such a low NSP intake.

- The constipation problem will continue if there is insufficient NSP and it may lead to other complications – e.g. haemorrhoids (piles) or diverticular disease.

- The elderly can become less active and this affects the movement of waste products in the intestine – i.e. it also slows down. For this reason a good supply of NSP is essential to ensure the effective and speedy removal of this waste.

Cleanliness is important in relation to health

Question 17

- Can be washed in warm water/40°C.

- A medium machine agitation/action should be used.

- The jacket should be rinsed, but with gradual cooling.

- The jacket can be spun at a reduced spin, or allowed to drip dry.

- A cool iron should be used/120°C.

- The jacket must not be bleached.

- The jacket can be dry cleaned using all solvents.

Question 18

Question 19

(a) and (b)

- Personal hygiene rules

The student was sneezing over the food because of hay fever.

Consequences:
Bacteria will be sprayed from the nose to the food. This may lead to food poisoning given the correct conditions.

The student did not have an apron to use when preparing the food.

Consequences:
Bacteria from the outer clothing of the student could be transferred to the food and so the food would become contaminated.

Using dish cloth as apron and then for drying dishes.

Consequences:
The dish cloth may have become contaminated with a variety of bacteria during the food preparation process. To then use this for drying clean dishes means that the bacteria will have spread to the dishes.

If the contaminated dishes are stored/used later bacteria may contaminate any food served on/in the dishes.

- Kitchen hygiene rules

Kitchen window was left open.

Consequences:
Flies/dirt/dust will be able to enter the kitchen via the window and contaminate any uncovered food/work surfaces with bacteria.

If uncovered food is eaten later, food poisoning may occur/if dirty work surfaces are used to prepare food, the food may become contaminated.

Placing hot dish into refrigerator.

Consequences:
The internal temperature of the fridge will be raised above 4°C and bacteria in food will be able to increase the rate of multiplication.

These foods may spoil/cause food poisoning if later consumed.

There may be contamination from raw to cooked foods within the fridge, depending on how the food was stored.

Question 20

The danger zone is the temperature zone between 5 and 63°C.

This is the temperature at which, given the correct conditions, bacteria can increase their rate of multiplication.

Question 21

Temperature
- The soup has been left in a warm kitchen and so will be stored within the danger zone (5–63°C).

- At this temperature bacteria, moulds and yeast may have been able to contaminate the soup and multiply given the warm temperature.

Food
- The soup is a good food source for micro organisms and, given a food supply and other correct conditions, these organisms can multiply.

- Bacteria in particular like protein foods and lentil soup will be a good source of protein.

Moisture
- The soup is a good source of moisture in the form of the stock in the soup. This – given that all the other conditions are present – will allow multiplication.

Oxygen
- If the soup has been left sitting all day it will have been open to air and so oxygen will have allowed aerobic bacteria to multiply.
- The action of the micro organisms (mould/yeast/bacteria) will have caused the soup to turn sour.

pH
- The soup will be at an ideal pH level to allow for bacterial multiplication – neither too acidic nor too alkaline.
- As the soup begins to spoil (the bacteria will multiply and produce some acid) the pH level of the soup will lower, making ideal conditions for mould and yeast growth.

Question 22

(a)

Freezing	Pickling/ chutney making	Jam making	Chilling	Vacuum packing
Apples	Apples	Apples	Apples	Apples †
Peas	Peas		Peas	Peas
Onions	Onions			Onions *
Strawberries		Strawberries	Strawberries	Strawberries
Cauliflower	Cauliflower		Cauliflower	Cauliflower
Cabbage	Cabbage		Cabbage	Cabbage *
Plums		Plums		
Brussel sprouts			Brussel sprouts	Brussel sprouts **

† Usually as part of a ready to eat fruit salad.

* Usually as part of a mixed salad pack.

** Usually fully prepared and ready to use.

(b) (i)
- Freezing reduces the storage temperature of the fish to below −18°C.
- This means that any water contained within the cells of the fish becomes frozen.
- If the water is frozen, it becomes unavailable for bacterial multiplication and so food spoilage is dramatically reduced.
- Any bacteria in the fish will become dormant (they cannot multiply) at this low temperature, so bacterial multiplication is stopped.

(ii)
- Packaging should be impervious to:
  - smell (to prevent the fish becoming tainted with the smell of other foods);
  - moisture (to prevent excessive water/ice surrounding the fish and damaging it).
- The packaging itself should not impart a smell or taste to the fish.
- The packaging must be able to prevent the strong smell of fish from tainting other foods being frozen.
- The packaging must be airtight, otherwise the fish will begin to dry slightly and affect the quality of the fish when defrosted.
- The packaging must not be too big for the product otherwise there will be excessive air surrounding the fish and this will dry it out slightly.

(c) Any five from:
- The raspberries will have to be individually placed on a tray to be frozen – this will prevent them from sticking together.
- Once frozen the individually frozen raspberries can be packed into small bags that can be later used and defrosted.
- Because the raspberries were individually frozen, the gardener can remove and use the exact quantity that he requires.
- The raspberries would be best frozen using the quick freeze facility of the freezer if available.
- Quick freezing means that the freezing temperature is reduced to at least −24°C. This means that smaller ice crystals will form.

22. (c) cont.

- If smaller ice crystals are formed, the raspberries are more likely to retain their shape and texture when freezing and so have good shape and texture when defrosted.
- The raspberries should only be stored for a limited amount of time. The longer the storage time, the poorer the quality of the end product when defrosted.
- The raspberries will have to be defrosted slowly in order to maintain their shape and texture.
- The raspberries should be labelled showing their weight and date of freezing. This will allow the gardener to check how long the product has been stored for.
- Only the best raspberries should be frozen. If they are already bruised or squashed they will not maintain their shape or texture when defrosted.

Question 23

Any five from:

- severe vomiting;
- diarrhoea;
- exhaustion;
- headache;
- fever;
- abdominal pain;
- tiredness.

Question 24

Action 1
- The centre of the chicken will still be frozen. The warmth of the oven will allow the centre to defrost slowly, but the chances are that it will not reach the required internal temperature of 75°C. This means that there is a risk of dangerous bacteria (e.g. Salmonella) multiplying in the chicken as it will have all the correct requirements – food, warmth, moisture and time.

Action 2
- This is a cross contamination situation. The raw chicken was prepared on the chopping board. This means that bacteria would be transferred from the chicken to the board. When the raw vegetables were prepared on the same board, there is a risk that bacteria from the board may have contaminated the raw vegetables. When eaten as part of the salad they may cause food poisoning.

Action 3
- The cheesecake was left to defrost by the window. Dirt, dust and insects may have landed on the cake when defrosting. This means that the cake was potentially contaminated with micro organisms. On defrosting the temperature of the cake will rise allowing the micro organisms to multiply. This may cause spoilage – if the cake is stored – or food poisoning if eaten.
- The cheesecake is also a very good source of food for bacteria as it is a high protein food (it has both cheese and cream as ingredients) and bacteria favour protein foods. The result will be spoilage and/or poisoning

Question 25

(a) Opened tin of beans
- Beans should have been removed from the tin, placed in a clean container and covered before being placed in the refrigerator.
- There will be a chemical reaction between the air and the lining of the tin which will cause the beans to spoil.
- The lid of the tin can will be very dangerous as it is sharp and it may cause an accident when removing items from the refrigerator.
- The beans will start to dry out and so spoil.
- The beans may become tainted with the smells/flavours of other foods as they are uncovered.

Bag of frozen peas
- The peas should be stored in the freezer and not the refrigerator because the refrigerator is not cold enough to ensure that the peas remain frozen.
- The temperature of the refrigerator will allow the peas to defrost and so possibly spoil.

Refrigerator temperature reading 9°C
- The internal temperature of the refrigerator is within the danger zone and so bacterial multiplication can start and foods stored within the refrigerator can begin to spoil.

Raw meat storage
- The meat is not covered and so may begin to dry out and spoil.
- The meat may become tainted with the smells/flavours of other foods as it is uncovered.
- The meat is not covered and blood/juices are dripping onto the food

below. This will contaminate the cooked food below and possibly cause food poisoning.

Mature cheddar cheese
- The use-by date of the cheese has been exceeded. The food is unsafe to eat as it is a perishable product.
- Food which has reached its use-by date should be disposed of.

Uncovered cheese
- The cheese is not covered and may start to dry out, causing it to spoil.
- The blood/juices from the meat may contaminate the uncovered cheese and cause illness if consumed.
- The cheese may become tainted with the smells/flavours of the other foods as it is uncovered.
- The cheese may cause other foods in the refrigerator to become tainted with the smell of cheese.

Mouldy cheese
- The mouldy cheese should be removed from the refrigerator as the mould can spread to other food.

Cooked pie – uncovered
- The pie is uncovered and so may dry out causing it to spoil.
- The meat pie may become tainted with the smells/flavours of other foods as it is uncovered.
- The cooked pie has meat juices/blood dripping onto it – this could cause illness/food poisoning if the pie is consumed.

Raw fish on plate
- The fish are not covered and so may begin to dry out and so spoil.
- The fish may become tainted with the smells/flavours of other foods as they are uncovered.
- The fish smell will certainly cause other foods in the refrigerator to become tainted with the odour of the fish.

General storage rules
- Cooked foods should be stored above uncooked foods so that any contamination from raw to cooked products can be prevented.

(b) Refrigerator should be regularly cleaned in order to:
- Remove any debris of food that may by lying in the refrigerator. These can

potentially attract micro organisms and so cause food spoilage/contamination.
- Remove any stale smells/odours that might be contained within the refrigerator. These odours can affect the taste/flavour of foods stored within the refrigerator.
- If the refrigerator is not cleaned on a regular basis, it may begin to operate less efficiently – e.g. food debris in the door seal may let cold air out of the fridge/warm air in.

(c) Freezer should be defrosted on a regular basis in order to:
- Reduce the amount of ice building up within the freezer. Should this happen, the freezer operates less efficiently and so is less economical to run/the internal temperature of the freezer may begin to rise.
- Remove any debris of food that may by lying in the freezer. These can potentially attract micro organisms and so cause food spoilage/contamination in the longer term.
- Remove any stale smells/odours that might be contained within the freezer. These odours can affect the taste/flavour of foods stored within the freezer.
- This will allow a check to be made on foods stored within the freezer. Foods that have been stored for longer than the suggested freeze time can be removed.

Safe working practices

Question 26

Picture 1
(a) Sharp knife lying on a work surface where children can pick it up.
(b) Cut
(c) • Knife removed to a safe place – e.g. lockable drawer, knife block/knife rack on wall.
- Do not leave sharp knife lying about.

Picture 2
(a) A child may drink the weed killer thinking it is lemonade.
(b) Poisoning
(c) • All garden chemicals should be left in a secure place – e.g. locked in a shed/left on an inaccessible shelf.
- Weed killers should be clearly labelled/not poured into lemonade bottles so that the contents can be mistaken.

26. cont.

Picture 3
(a)   The stool may fall over/break/collapse knocking the lady over.

(b)   Fall

(c)
- Step ladders/secure steps should be used to reach for items on high shelves/cupboards.
- Commonly used items should not be stored in inaccessible places.
- The old lady should ask for assistance if she needs to obtain items from high places.

Picture 4
(a)   A child could reach for the iron and so injure itself/knock it over.

(b)   Scald/burn

(c)
- Irons should never be left unattended when there are children.
- Children's toys should not be left near dangerous items because they may attract infants to the items and so increase the possibility of an accident.

Picture 5
(a)   There is a frayed wire on the food processor which can be dangerous.

The flex is trailing over a sink of water. If the frayed flex dips into the water it will be dangerous.

(b)   Electrocution

(c)
- Have the flex on the appliance repaired.
- Dispose of the appliance and buy a new one.
- Do not use an appliance anywhere near water/select a different electrical socket to use – well away from the sink.

Question 27

- Young children tend to be more curious/less aware of the dangers around them and so are more likely to be involved in accidents.
- The elderly can be less co-ordinated/may have poor eyesight/ hearing and so may be more likely to be involved in an accident.

Question 28

(a)   Any five from:
- Switch the blenders on at the socket using dry hands only.
- Read the instructions before use.
- Do not immerse fully in water when cleaning/do not place in a dishwasher.
- Switch off the power source after use.
- Do not clean the blades when the power is switched on.

- Care should be taken when blending hot products to prevent splashing.
- Ensure the product is switched off if adding or removing attachments.
- When storing the blender after use, return it to its packaging to prevent the blades causing an accident when the blender is removed from the cupboard/storage area.
- Do not use the blender if it has a damaged/frayed/kinked flex.

(b)   This means that the blender does not have an earth wire. Because of this, the product has been designed to ensure that the risks of getting an electrical shock when using it are minimised.

Design features

Question 29

Any four from:
Cost
- The cost of the jeans will have to fit in with the budget available.
- The method of payment accepted by the shop may determine how much can be paid for the jeans – e.g. if lacking in cash, but using a credit card, the price might not be so important.

Size/age/shape
- The size of the jeans will have to be considered to ensure they are a good fit.
- The shape/age of the teenager will have to be considered – e.g. if they are very tall a longer leg will be required.

Style/likes and dislikes/colour
- The likes and dislikes of the teenager will be important in determining the style to be selected.
- The occasion for which the jeans are to be used will determine the style to be bought – e.g. casual for everyday wear or styled for special occasions.
- A teenager might be keen to buy jeans that feature a designer label/be similar to that of friends and so would have to be considered.
- The colour would have to be one that met with the likes and needs of the teenager.

Existing wardrobe
- What the teenager has that would coordinate with the jeans would have to be considered to ensure that the jeans were worn/so there were no additional demands for purchases to coordinate with the jeans.

Location

- The type of shopping outlets available to purchase clothing may determine what range of jeans are available and so affect choice.
- If selection of clothing is a problem due to location, mail order catalogues may offer an opportunity to look at a wide range of jeans by parent and teenager together.
- Mail order may offer the ability to pay for the jeans over a period of time which may be important if money is short.

Fabric

- The type of fabric used to make the jeans will be important for the following reasons:
- To ensure that the fabric is comfortable against the skin so that the jeans will be worn.
- Some specialist jeans are made from fabrics which are dry clean only and this would need to be considered in terms of additional costs and inconvenience.
- A fabric that will be able to withstand washing/regular wear might be important if the jeans are going to be worn often.
- Ease of washing in terms of dye running from the jeans will have to be considered as this would mean having to wash the jeans on their own and this can add to overall cost considerations.

Occasion

- If it is for a birthday, then the parent will want to ensure that the jeans are special and so he would consider a wide range of the factors identified above.

Question 30

Any six from:

3 piece outfit

- The trousers and T-shirt can be worn on warmer days/when baby is warm.
- The cardigan can be use when it is cooler/ baby is cold.
- The three items co-ordinate so, no matter what combination is used, the items will go well together.
- The three piece outfit can be used when the baby has to look smart/the two piece outfit may look more causal when required.

Cotton T-shirt with press stud fastening

- The cotton is absorbent and so will make the baby feel comfortable as sweat will be absorbed.
- Cotton is a comfortable fabric against the skin so will not irritate the baby.

- The fleece type cotton fabric will trap air and so allow for the retention of warmth for the baby.
- The press stud fastening will allow for ease of dressing/undressing the baby.
- The studs should not irritate the baby when wearing the T-shirt.
- May be more secure than buttons and so are safer/there is less risk of baby detaching and chewing them.

Printed logo on T-shirt

- This type of design is currently fashionable and so the baby will look 'trendy'/smart/fashionable.
- The logo is in a colour that will match with the other items in the set and so the baby will look smart/co-ordinated.

Fleece type zip front cardigan with hood

- The fleece type fabric will trap air and so allow for the retention of warmth for the baby.
- The zip front will allow for ease of dressing/undressing the baby.
- The zip front will allow for added protection from cold when baby is outside/ it is cooler.
- The hood can be used to insulate the head and so maintain warmth when it is cold/ baby is outside.

Fleece type trousers with elasticated waist

- The fleece type fabric will trap air and so allow for the retention of warmth for the baby.
- The elasticated waistband will allow for ease of dressing and undressing the baby.
- The elasticated waist will allow for some degree of growth and so trousers may last longer.
- The elasticated waist will allow for some freedom of movement and so the baby will be more comfortable.

Inverted pleats on trouser knees

- This will allow for freedom of movement – which is important as babies like to kick legs/be active.
- It is an added design feature that would make the outfit look different and so appeal.

Colours

- The outfit comes in a variety of colours that will suit both boys and girls.

Sizes

- The outfit comes in a range of sizes and so it should not be difficult to get an outfit that will fit.

Question 31

This is an evaluation type question, so you should talk about all the good and bad points of the trousers.

100% cotton
- Cotton is an absorbent fabric and so this will absorb sweat. This is good as the chef will be working in warm conditions.
- Cotton is a durable/strong fibre and so will withstand the constant wear and tear/stretching to which the trousers will be subjected.
- Cotton is not very flame resistant and so if he buys the trousers without the special finish, they may be dangerous/be a safety hazard.
- Cotton has good laundering properties and so this is an advantage as the trousers will need to be washed on a very regular basis to ensure food safety.

Baggy design
- The trousers are of a baggy design and this means that they will allow for freedom of movement as the chef will be stretching/bending.
- The trousers are of a baggy design and this means that the chef may be more comfortable because if he does become warm, the trousers will not cling to him, but allow for evaporation of perspiration from the legs and so cool him down.
- The baggy design may mean that the fabric gets caught on work surfaces and so tear/cause an accident/be a safety hazard.

Extra soft finish
- The chef may be wearing the trousers for a long period of time and with lots of bending and stretching the trousers should not irritate him. As they have a soft finish this should not be a problem.

Two side pockets and one back pocket
- This allows the chef to carry a variety of objects safely – e.g. coins, wallet – as it might not be safe to leave them lying about.
- The chef can carry items that he might require during the day – e.g. supplier phone numbers, recipe cards.
- This might encourage the chef to carry items such as handkerchiefs that are really not suitable for using in a kitchen and so compromise food safety.

Tapered legs
- This is a good safety feature as it means that there will be no loose fabric that he might trip over or catch and so it adds to safety.

Elasticated waist with drawstring
- The elasticated waist means that the trousers will accommodate a small increase in weight/allow for comfort in wearing.
- The elasticated waist means that the garment will be able to accommodate the stretching and bending that a chef might have to do and so add to comfort/help them last longer.
- The drawstring means that the trousers can be adjusted to accommodate different waist sizes, so aiding comfort.
- The drawstring may reduce the amount of flexibility/movement of the chef and so reduce comfort.

Available in 6 different designs
- The chef can select a design that best suits his likes and dislikes.
- The chef can select a 'trendy'/modern design that might appeal to his student customers.
- The chef may wish for a more traditional design, which is not available and so may not suit his needs/likes.
- The designs come in a variety of colours and so he can choose one that matches his likes.
- The chef may decide to select dark coloured trousers/design, thinking that it may not show up dirt and stains as much and so food safety may be compromised.

Available with a special flame-resistant finish
- This is a good feature as he will be working near naked flames and so a fire-resistant finish will be a good safety feature.
- Cotton has low flame resistance and so this finish will improve the functionality/design of the trousers.
- The flame-resistant finish is an extra that will cost additional money and so he would need to consider this before buying.

Question 32

(a) and (b)

(i) Electric washing machine

Reduce the washing temperature to 40°C/lower if possible.

- This will reduce the amount of energy required to heat the water to a higher temperature.

Use the half/reduced wash facility for smaller loads.

- This means that less energy will be used in the washing process.

Use the economy cycle.

- The water temperature of the wash is automatically reduced and so energy is saved as the water will not need to be heated to as high a temperature.

Switch off the machine after use.

- Although the machine is not washing clothes, it will still be using energy.

Use during off-peak time.

- If the machine has a time delay button/function the wash can be set to go on during the night when energy is cheaper.
- Put the machine on last thing at night so off-peak energy can be used – which is cheaper.

Use a reduced spin if appropriate.

- This will use less energy rotating the machine drum.

Use the quick wash facility if available

- This shortens the washing cycle and so saves energy in the long term.

(ii)   Dishwasher

Use during off-peak time.

- If the machine has a time delay button/function the wash can be set to go on during the night when energy is cheaper.
- Put the machine on last thing at night so off-peak energy can be used – which is cheaper.

Use the quick wash facility if available.

- This shortens the washing cycle and so saves energy in the long term.

Reduce the washing temperature if possible.

- This will reduce the amount of energy required to heat the water to a higher temperature.

Use the economy cycle.

- The water temperature of the wash is automatically reduced and so energy is saved as the water will not need to be heated to as high a temperature.

Use the half/reduced wash facility for smaller loads.

- This means that less energy will be used in the washing process.

Switch off the machine after use.

- Although the machine is not washing dishes, it will still be using energy.
- Only using the machine when it is full saves energy on small loads.

Question 33

(a)
- The clear view inside will allow someone who is hard of hearing to be able to see when the kettle is boiling as they may have difficulty hearing when boiling has started.
- The illumination during boiling will allow the hard of hearing person to identify when the kettle is boiling as they may have difficulty hearing when it is boiling.
- The flashing LEDs will allow the hard of hearing person to identify when the kettle is on standby and so keeping the water warm.
- The indicators will alert the hard of hearing person to the fact that the kettle has been switched off at the mains/the kettles is switched on.

Note: Not all the features will be of benefit to the hard of hearing.

(b)
- The ability to keep the water warm would be useful if the office has to provide tea/coffee to visitors/for meetings.
- The ability to rapid boil will be useful when coffee/tea is required quickly for the office coffee break.
- The clear view inside will allow the office staff to see when the kettle is boiling as they may have difficulty hearing if the office is busy/noisy.
- The illumination during boiling will allow the office staff to identify when the kettle is boiling as they may have difficulty hearing when it is boiling due to office noise/if the office is busy.
- The flashing LEDs will allow someone working in the office to identify when the kettle is on standby and keeping the water warm.
- The rotating base means that the kettle can be adjusted easily so that no one in the office will knock it and cause an accident.
- The kettle is cordless and so this is a good safety feature as it means there is no trailing flexes that could be a safety hazard in an office.

Question 34

(a)   Model B

Any eight reasons from:

Condenser
- This will be used at the back of a room and this type is suitable as it does not require to be vented via an outside wall.

34. (a) cont.

- This type can be used in almost any place as the water is contained within the machine. This makes it suitable for using at the back of the class room.

Cost
- This is the second cheapest but, given the added features, this would make it good value for money.

Fuel used
- This model uses only electricity and so meets the needs of the department in that the place it will be located has an available electricity power socket.

Drying capacity
- This model has the largest drying capacity and so suits the needs of a Home Economics Department as it will be used on a regular basis and will have large loads of cloths and towels.

Heat settings
- This has two heat settings and so the Home Economics Department can dry other items in the dryer that require a different heat setting.

Drying time
- This model has the quickest drying time. This is good as it means the cloths can be dried quickly for classes to use/cloths can be dried quickly and the Home Economics Department will have a lot to dry each day.
- The drying time is the quickest and so the running costs should be lower which is good as the Home Economics Department is on a tight budget.

Noise level
- This has the lowest noise level and so will be good for the Home Economics Department as it will be placed at the back of a classroom and so should not disturb the class when working.

Energy rating
- This is the best energy rating of the three models. This means that it will be the most energy efficient when drying and so suit the tight budget of the Home Economics Department.

Colour
- This model only comes in white. This should not be a problem for the Home Economics Department as colour coordination will not be as important as it would be for a fitted kitchen/home purchase.

Filter
- This will be used by both staff and pupils and the easy accessible filter means that it can be changed easily/cleaned easily.

Reverse action drying
- This means that the drying time is speeded up so saving time when drying. This means that the towels and cloths will be dried quicker/available to use by classes quicker.
- The reverse action will mean that the dishcloths and towels will not tangle and so they should be easy to fold for the staff/pupils.

Final cool tumble
- The cool down period will mean that the cloths and towels will not be badly creased and so can be used by classes quickly/soon after drying.

(b)   Model C.

Question 35

Ironing Board 3

Any four reasons from:

Solid steel top
- The solid steel top is the most durable/is the strongest type and the students want a model that is durable/will last a long time.
- Students may be careless with the board and, if it is solid steel, it will be more difficult to damage.

Size
- This is the second smallest and so should be easy to store and this is what they are looking for.

Height adjustable
- This ironing board can be adjusted and this should suit the students as it can be adjusted to suit their different heights/requirements.

Folded height
- The folded height is second smallest and so this will mean that it should be easy to fold away and store which is what the students want.

Guarantee
- The guarantee is for 10 years, indicating the manufacturer's faith in the product's durability, which is what the students want.
- The guarantee means that if the ironing board frame becomes faulty, it will be replaced/repaired which is good as the students are putting their money together and so will have no further outlay.

Price
- This model is not the cheapest but it is not the most expensive. This means that when the students club together the cost per student will be minimal.
- Not the cheapest but offers best value for money to suit their needs.

Free sleeve board
- This is a good feature for the students as two of the students have to wear shirts on their work placement and this added feature will assist them in this task/will make their shirts look smart for the work placement.

Question 36

Cost of £198·00
- Sandy can afford this iron as she has a £400 grant for equipment and this will leave some money for other equipment.

Vertical steam
- If Sandy gets items such as curtains to iron, she can steam these from a hanging position which might make the task easier.
- If she is planning a mobile ironing business then the vertical steam facility will be useful if she has to iron curtains on site.
- This feature might not be one of the most important features, depending on what types of ironing she will accept.

5-minute heat up
- This is quite a long heat up period for an iron and this might slow down her ironing progress if she has to wait for the iron to heat up each time it is switched on.
- There is no indication as to whether this is a long time for an iron to heat up or not and so this may in fact not be a problem.

Lightweight
- The fact that the iron is lightweight is good as it means her wrist will not tire quickly and so she will get more ironing done/will not damage her wrist.
- If the iron is very light it may affect its performance in terms of ability to remove creases and this would slow down the pace of ironing.

Anti-scale solution available
- This is a good feature as the anti-scale solution will prevent lime building up inside the iron and so extend the life of the iron. Being a business this will save her money in the long term.
- The solution is available implying that it has to be purchased. Sandy would have to consider the cost of this when budgeting for the business.
- Sandy has some of her equipment grant left and she could use part of this money to buy the solution.

- May not be needed if living in a soft-water area, so saving money.

Free loan service
- For a business this is a good offer because if the iron breaks down the business will not be able to operate and so profits will be affected.
- Sandy would have to wait up to 24 hours before getting a replacement iron and in this time she might lose business/not be able to fulfil her ironing work which may lead to unhappy customers.

Easy to fill removable tank
- This is a good feature as it means Sandy can iron for up to $1 \frac{1}{2}$ hours at a time without having to stop to replace the water so more ironing can be done.
- The tank is removable which is good as it means it can be filled with water away from the electrical components of the iron and so is safe for Sandy to use.
- The tank is easy to fill and will save Sandy time and effort so she can concentrate on ironing/not spilling water over electrical components/client's ironing when filling.

5× steam power
- This feature means that the ironing should be quicker and so Sandy will be able to get a lot of ironing done in a shorter period of time.
- The added steam power means that difficult creases can be ironed out more quickly and so the ironing will be done quicker.
- The steam would be able to give sharp and clear creases to garments where required and so might please customers and encourage them to come back.

Ultra glide sole plate
- This feature will make ironing less energetic/tiring on the arm and so will mean that Sandy can iron more clothes per hour than if using a standard iron.
- This feature will make ironing less tiring on the arm and so help prevent any muscle damage to her arm.
- This will help prevent damage to the clothes she is ironing as the sole plate is smooth.
- Implies that the iron will iron smoothly and so there is less chance of damage to the clothing through burning.

Question 37

- Elastane has poor absorbency and so the swimming outfit will not soak up water so helping with swimming performance.
- Elastane has poor absorbency and so this assists in the drying process as less water is absorbed.
- Elastane is a very durable fibre and so this will help the swimming outfit last for a longer period of time.

37 cont.

- Elastane is a strong fibre and so this will ensure that the stretching and straining that occurs when swimming will not damage the outfit.

- Elastane is very resistant to creasing and this means that the outfit will not require much attention once washed.

- Elastane is very elastic and so the outfit will hug close to the body, preventing drag and so improving swimming performance.

- Elastane is very elastic and so the outfit will be able to return quickly to its shape even after much washing and stretching.

- Elastane is very easy to wash and this is important as swimming outfits need to be washed after swimming to remove the chlorine which can damage fibres.

Question 38

FIBRE INFORMATION CHART

Fibre	Natural or synthetic?	Strong or weak?	Flammable or non-flammable?	Absorbent or non-absorbent?	Easy or difficult to wash?
Cotton	Natural	Strong	Flammable	Absorbent	Easy
Nylon	Synthetic	Strong	Non-flammable	Non-absorbent	Easy
Wool	Natural	Weak	Non-flammable	Absorbent	Difficult
Silk	Natural	Strong	Non-flammable	Absorbent	Difficult
Elastane	Synthetic	Strong	Flammable	Non-absorbent	Easy

Physical needs of individuals and families

Question 39

(a) Washable

- The garment can be washed at a high temperature which is good as the jacket will become dirty easily as it is for a mechanic.

- The jacket may become stained with oil/grease/dirt and so it needs to be washed at a high temperature to remove stains.

- If the jacket is able to be washed at a high temperature to remove stains/ washed regularly it will mean that the mechanic will have a good appearance when assisting motorists.

- If the jacket is able to be washed regularly it means that the high visibility colour will be maintained and so ensures safety at the roadside/ ensures high visibility at the roadside.

High visibility
- The outer jacket has high visibility and this is important to the mechanic who needs to be assured that other road users can see him if he is repairing a vehicle on the roadside.

- Alerts motorists to his presence on the road so that they can slow down/take care in the area where the breakdown has taken place.

Detachable outer
- This is good because if it is a warm day the inner jacket can be removed ensuring comfort, but the high-visibility outer can still be worn so motorists can spot him/ensures his safety.

- The inner jacket may be restrictive in terms of movement when repairing a car and so, if it can be removed and the high-visibility outer worn, it will make his job easier and ensure his safety.

Microporous liner
- This is good as the liner is breathable and waterproof and so this means that when the mechanic is repairing vehicles in bad weather, he will be able to feel dry and comfortable.

- Should the mechanic begin to feel warm when repairing vehicles, the breathable liner will draw moisture from his body so ensuring that he feels comfortable when working.

Badges
- The outer can have the company badge sewn on to it meaning that the mechanic can be identified as a member of a particular repair company.
- Having the ability to have your own badge sewn on to the outer may mean that the customer feels safer if the mechanic can be identified as belonging to a particular vehicle breakdown company.
- The company badge would act as a form of advertising for the mechanic when out on breakdowns/when wearing the jacket.

Pockets
- The availability of pockets is ideal for the mechanic as he will have to carry items such as pen/notebook/tools etc to the roadside from his vehicle.
- The mechanic can leave valuables (e.g. money) in the internal zipped pockets rather than leaving the money in his van and so this is safer/more secure.

Jacket length
- The jacket length is at upper thigh level. This means that on colder days he will have full upper body protection against the wind and rain and so assist him in his work.
- The jacket will protect some of his inner clothing if he has to go under a vehicle as it offers total upper body cover.

Velcro® fastening cuffs
- These can be adjusted to suit the size of the mechanic's wrists so providing comfort when working.
- The Velcro® fastening means that the cuffs can be adjusted easily and, if he has cold hands, this style of fastening will make this easier.
- The Velcro® fastening means that draughts can be prevented, ensuring comfort in his work.

Velcro® front closing
- The Velcro® fastening means that the jacket can be opened/closed easily and, if it is cold weather, this style of closing will assist with this process.

(b) and (c)
Possible additional features include:
Elasticated waist
- This would prevent draughts from penetrating the jacket (particularly when the weather is poor) and so would keep him warm/comfortable.

- This would not only prevent draughts but still allow for flexibility of movement when working.

Outer pockets to be zipped/Velcro® fastened
- This would allow for the storage of items (e.g. notebooks) and would ensure that they did not fall out when the mechanic was undertaking vehicle repair work.

High level collar
- A high level collar would mean that the neck of the mechanic would be kept warm/dry when he was repairing vehicles in poor weather.

Detachable hood
- This would be good for the mechanic when he has to work in poor weather conditions as it would keep him dry and so make him feel more comfortable/hood could be used when weather was bad, giving some protection from the elements.
- The hood can be removed in warm weather to prevent it getting in the way when working

Front opening
- This could be zipped rather than Velcro® as the movements that a mechanic would make may cause the Velcro® to open.

Question 40

(a) Fastenings
- The fastening would need to be of a suitable size and shape to encourage the toddler to use them.
- Toddlers tend to want to be independent and so selecting a suitable fastening that can be used by a toddler would help him/her to dress and undress.
- The fastenings would need to be safe for the toddler – e.g. if the toddler was to fall large/obtrusive fastening may hurt him/her.
- Fastenings would need to be durable as a toddler's clothing tends to be washed on a regular basis.
- The style of clothing will determine the most suitable fastening to be selected and so will need to be considered when designing.

(b) Size
- Toddlers come in all sorts of shapes and sizes and so the designer will need to consider what sizes should be catered for.

40. (b) cont.

- There may be features that he/she can add to the trousers to assist in sizing – e.g. an elasticated waistband.
- The sizes that will be designed will affect the amount of fabric used and so the end cost.

(c) Absorbency
- Toddlers tend to be quite active and so using fabric that will absorb perspiration/moisture will make the toddler feel comfortable.
- May stain more easily so fabric will have to withstand extra washing.

(d) Stretch
- Toddlers tend to be quite active and so using fabric that will stretch with body movements will be comfortable for the toddler.
- Toddlers tend to be quite active and so using fabric that will stretch with body movements will not hinder movement/flexibility.
- Fastenings/threads/construction techniques will need to be selected that will suit the nature of the stretch fabric used.

(e) Safety
- Toddlers tend to be active/curious and so the trousers will need to be designed to ensure that safety is paramount.
- The fastenings would need to be safe for the toddler – e.g. if the toddler was to fall large/obtrusive fastening may hurt him/her/fastenings would need to have no sharp objects.
- Elasticated leg bottoms may assist by ensuring that there is no excess fabric at leg bottoms on trousers designed for active wear. If they were too baggy, the child may trip up/catch clothing and fall.
- Flame resistance is an important property that the designer would have to consider. Selecting fabric that did not burn easily would be important in case the child came into contact with a naked flame.
- Cord fastenings on waistbands may pose a risk in terms of catching on objects, causing a child to fall/injure himself.

Question 41

Shelter	Description
1	C
2	F
3	B
4	A
5	D
6	E

Question 42

(a)
- Citizen's Advice Bureau;
- Consumer Advice Centre;
- Consumer Protection Department.

(b) Environmental Health Department is best choice, but you could go to Citizen's Advice Bureau or the Consumer Advice Centre.

(c) Consumers' Association.

(d)
- Citizen's Advice Bureau;
- Consumer Advice Centre;
- Consumer Protection Department.

(e) Environmental Health Department is best choice, but you could go to Citizen's Advice Bureau or the Consumer Advice Centre.

(f) Environmental Health Department is best choice, but you could go to Citizen's Advice Bureau or the Consumer Advice Centre.

(g) Consumer Protection Department is the best choice, but you could go to Citizen's Advice Bureau or the Consumer Advice Centre.

(h) Environmental Health Department.

(i) Consumer Protection Department is the best choice but you could go to Citizen's Advice Bureau or the Consumer Advice Centre.

(j) Citizen's Advice Bureau or the Consumer Advice Centre.

(k) Consumers' Association.

(l) Consumer Protection Department is the best choice, but you could go to the Citizens Advice Bureau or the Consumer Advice Centre.

(m) Scottish Consumer Council.

Question 43

(a) and (b)

Situation 1
Sale and Supply of Goods Act 1994
- The suitcase is not of 'satisfactory quality' because the wheels fell off when first used.
- Mr Smith is entitled to a refund of his money.

Situation 2
Sale and Supply of Goods Act 1994
- The drill is not 'as described' as it has parts missing.

- Mr Smith is entitled to a refund of his money because even though he bought it in the sale it should have been a complete set.
- If the item was labelled as 'incomplete' when purchased, Mr Smith would have no protection.

Trade Descriptions Act 1968 and 1972
- This might apply depending on how the product was described. If described as a complete set, but in fact the store knew that parts were missing, an offence has been committed.

Situation 3
Sale and Supply of Goods Act 1994
- The phone is not 'as described'/'fit for purpose' as it does not do specifically what Mr Smith had requested.
- Mr Smith is entitled to a refund of his money.

Trade Descriptions Act 1968 and 1972
- This would apply as the product has been falsely described to Mr Smith.

Situation 4
Sale and Supply of Goods Act 1994
- The trousers are not 'as described', i.e. they are not waterproof.
- Mr Smith is entitled to a refund of his money.

Trade Descriptions Act 1968 and 1972
- This would apply as the product has been falsely described to Mr Smith.

Situation 5
Food Safety (Temperature Control) Regulations 1995
- This states that chilled foods (the cream cakes) must be stored at temperatures below 8°C in order to prevent bacterial growth.

Food Safety Act 1990
- The salmon is not as stated – i.e. it is Welsh farmed salmon and not Fresh Scottish salmon – and so the supermarket is breaking the Food Safety Act.

The Sale and Supply of Goods Act 1994 and the Trades Descriptions Act 1968 and 1972 may also apply here as they also cover false product descriptions.

Situation 6
Food Hygiene (General) Regulations 1995 and Food Safety (General Food Hygiene) Regulations 1995
- These regulations deal with the general hygiene requirements of food premises, including cafés. Having a caged bird in a kitchen would not meet with the requirements of the regulations.

Question 44
(a) (i) and (ii)
Any five from:

Ingredients list
- This will allow the consumer to compare similar products in terms of quantities of different ingredients in each product.

- It will allow the consumer to see if the product contains ingredients that they might be allergic to/not like.
- Allows consumers to follow a healthy diet where sugar, fat and salt appear low on the list or not at all.

Product name/description
- This will let the consumer know what they are buying.
- It will let the consumer know what flavour/colour the product is (i.e. Orange jelly).

Indication of shelf-life
- This lets the consumer know how long the product will remain in good quality/how long it can be stored.
- Indicates to the consumer when the product should be disposed of.
- Can allow the consumer to make comparisons about the shelf life of similar products.

Product weight
- Allows the consumer to make comparisons between similar products/ allows value for money comparisons.
- Allows the consumer to ascertain the quantity of product held within the container.
- The 'e' symbol must be placed beside the weight if the 'average' weight is given and not the specific weight.

Name and address of manufacturer
- This is useful for the consumer in case they have a complaint that they need to refer to the company.
- It is useful for a consumer who may not wish to buy a product produced by a specific company.

Origin of product
- Consumers may not wish to buy/may prefer to buy products from a specific country and so this information would assist them with product choice.

Instructions for use
- For this product instructions for use have to be provided because the product is not usually used in the purchased form – i.e. water has to be added. This ensures that the product is used correctly and so the consumer does not waste their money/become ill through incorrect preparation.

Storage conditions
- If a product has specific storage requirements to ensure that it remains in good condition and safe to eat, these have to be stated on the label.

44. cont.

(b) (i) and (ii)
Any three from:

Nutritional labelling
- This is not compulsory (it is given in this product) but when it is provided, the manufacturer has to follow specific guidance on what information must be provided.

Serving suggestion/serving tip/recipe provided for jelly slurp
- This is not compulsory, but it does give the consumer different ideas for using the product and different methods of presenting the product.

Bar code
- This is not compulsory and will not really affect the consumer. It is a mechanism for the shop to electronically mark the price of goods and this information is linked to their tills.
- This is mainly used by the shop as a means of recording the sale of products so that items sold can be re-ordered.
- Bar codes are used by some shops to allow the consumer to electronically scan the goods they buy, allowing them to keep a running total of what they have spent.

Recycling symbol
- This is used by the manufacturer to indicate that the packaging is either made of recycled materials (card) or can be recycled. If the consumer is environmentally minded, this information will be useful to them.

Consumer Services details
- This is not compulsory but it does provide the consumer with a phone number that they can use should they require further information about the product and so may encourage the consumer to buy the product knowing they have a contact point once the product has been bought.

Question 45

(a) and (b)

Alcohol
- Alcohol has a high energy value and excessive intake can lead to a person being overweight and so the chances of heart disease are increased.
- Alcohol is a type of chemical and so can affect the heart in many other ways, with the end result being heart-failure.

Smoking
- Cigarettes contain a large amount of chemicals and so can affect the heart in many ways, with the end result being heart-failure.
- The arteries leading to the heart can become blocked resulting in coronary thrombosis which leads to heart disease.

Drugs
- Drugs are chemicals which can affect your body in many different ways but many will eventually affect your heart.
- Short term side effects include increased or reduced heart rate/heart flutters, whilst longer term effects include heart-failure.

Stress
- Stress is associated with high blood pressure and this in turn can be linked to heart-failure/disease.

Insufficient exercise
- Our bodies should have an energy balance. What energy we intake via food, we should use up via activity. If we do not take sufficient exercise, excess energy is stored as fat in the body. This is associated with heart disease.

High blood pressure
- This is where the arteries carrying the blood are working at very high pressure. This puts a strain on the heart and can lead to heart-failure.

Family history
- There is a link between different generations of the same family. If your parents suffered from heart disease, your chances of having heart disease may be increased.

Age
- The older you are, the longer your heart has had to work. Your heart will work less and less efficiently and eventually will stop altogether.

Question 46

Smock
- The smock is ideal for summer wear as it has a high percentage of cotton which makes it a comfortable fabric to wear.
- The cotton content will mean that the smock will be able to absorb moisture/perspiration and so make the wearer feel comfortable./It is summer and the wearer may perspire and the cotton content of the smock will be able to absorb some moisture and so aid comfort.

- The elastane content of the smock means that this garment will have some stretch which will be required by the pregnant woman as her pregnancy develops.
- The elastane will give the garment good stretch recovery/shape retention and so the garment can be worn again and again without going out of shape.
- Garments for pregnant women should not feel restrictive when worn. This has 2% elastane in it and so will allow for freedom of movement when stretching/bending.
- The V-neck will allow the wearer to feel cool in the summer months and so aid comfort.
- The V-neck will add to the feeling of freedom of movement and so aid comfort.
- The $^3/_4$ length sleeves will allow the wearer to feel cool in summer months.
- If the summer months are cold and wet, this style of smock may not be ideal.
- The slits on the hem and sleeves will allow additional freedom of movement and so make the wearer feel more comfortable.
- There is a range of colours and prints available and so the woman should be able to select a colour that suits her.
- The colours/patterns are quite bright and so would not suit a woman looking for darker colours.
- This style of garment may not suit all tastes and so may not be purchased.
- There is a wide variety of sizes available and so the wearer should have no problems finding a smock that will fit.

Trousers
- The stretch front mesh panel will allow the woman to wear the trousers and not feel it digging into her stomach.
- The stretch panel will accommodate the increase in weight that the woman will be experiencing and so will aid comfort.
- The adjustable elastic means that the trousers can be adjusted to suit the stage of pregnancy and so aid comfort.
- The button fastening will allow for a feeling of security in terms of a good fit.
- The button fastening may not be a good idea as it may press into the stomach and so feel uncomfortable.
- The trousers only come in one leg size and so this may not suit tall or short women.
- The trousers come in a range of average waist sizes and so most women should be able to get a pair of trousers that fit well.
- The trousers do not come in a size above 18 and so, if the pregnant woman was a size 20 or 22, she would be able to buy a smock, but not trousers.

- There is a small range of bright colours that would suit summer time.
- The colour range is limited and would not always allow for a good match with the smock.

Management of expenditure

Question 47

A balanced budget is one where the total expenditure (spending) of a household is equal to the total income (money coming in) of the household.

Question 48

(a)   Cash

Advantages
- Mr and Mrs Jones can only buy what they can afford and so they do not go into debt.
- It is an easy method of purchasing goods/everybody accepts cash.
- Mr and Mrs Jones may be able to negotiate a discount if paying by cash.

Disadvantages
- This is a large amount of money to carry around and it could be easily lost/stolen.
- If Mr and Mrs Jones do not have £299·99 in cash they cannot buy the dishwasher.

(b)   Credit card

Advantages
- Mr and Mrs Jones do not have to carry £299·99 cash around with them and so it is possibly safer/more convenient.
- They can purchase the dishwasher with the credit card and, if they pay it back in sufficient time, they will pay no interest.
- This is an expensive item to purchase and so they may have added consumer protection should anything happen to the dishwasher at a later date.
- If bought by credit card, it can assist with budgeting if a set amount is put by each month to pay off the £299·99.
- There may be additional rewards for paying by credit card – e.g. air miles/ reward points.
- Most stores accept credit cards and so this is a suitable method of purchase.

Disadvantages
- Mr and Mrs Jones may not be able to afford the dishwasher, but may purchase it with the card and so may get into debt.

48 (b). cont.

- If the full amount is not paid off within a specified period, interest will be charged on the balance.
- Cards can be stolen and used fraudulently.
- Not everyone can get credit and so this form of payment may not be available.

(c) Credit sale

Advantages

- Mr and Mrs Jones do not have to carry £299·99 in cash around with them and so it is possibly safer/more convenient.
- This is an expensive item to purchase and so they may have added consumer protection should anything happen to the dishwasher at a later date.
- Interest-free credit may be available meaning that no additional charges will be incurred.
- Most stores offer credit sale agreements and so obtaining this should not be a problem.
- These agreements often have fixed monthly payments and so can assist when preparing a monthly budget.

Disadvantages

- Mr and Mrs Jones may not be able to afford the dishwasher, but may purchase it on credit and so may get into debt.
- Not everyone can get credit and so this form of payment may not be available.

Question 49

- The student should look for some advice – e.g. from the Citizen's Advice Bureau, Consumer Advice Centre, bank or building society, Consumer Credit and Counselling Service.
- The student must speak/communicate with all his creditors to ensure that they are aware of his current financial situation.
- The student should not ignore the problem as it will not go away – indeed it would make things worse.
- An income and expenditure sheet should be drawn up to allow the student to get a realistic idea of the current situation.

  This information should be given to the advisor or creditors so that they will be able to understand the student's situation.
- The student should see what steps can be taken to reduce his non-essential spending and then make a realistic offer of payment to the creditors.

- The list of creditors should be prioritised – e.g. if the rent is not paid, the student may become homeless. These areas may need to get immediate/highest payments.
- The student must stick to any payment agreements that are made with creditors, otherwise they may ask for full and immediate payment/take court action to recover debt.

Question 50

(a) (i) Fixed
- Mortgage;
- Insurance;
- Council tax;
- Road tax;
- Car insurance;
- TV License;
- Loans/credit cards;
- Club memberships;
- Nursery fees.

(ii) Variable

- Food;
- Clothing;
- Maintenance of house;
- Electricity;
- Gas;
- Toiletries and household goods;
- Car running costs;
- Telephone;
- Mobile phone;
- Savings;
- Travelling expenses;
- Entertaining;
- Holidays;
- Birthdays and Christmas.

(b) This budget can be regarded as a balanced budget as the amount of income and the amount of expenditure is balanced. This is good.

The budget has been worked out to ensure that funds are put aside for all major areas of expenditure and includes savings – that could be used for a 'rainy day'.

(c) and (d)

Areas of non-essential expenditure should be examined first, before looking at essential areas.

Holiday money
- Spending on holidays should be stopped in this period as this money can be used to pay some of the essential bills.
- Any savings accumulated in this area may have to be used to pay essential bills.
- Holidays may have to be cancelled in order to make savings to pay essential bills.

Birthdays and Christmas money
- Spending on birthdays and Christmas money should be stopped in this period as this money can be used to pay some of the essential bills.

- Any savings accumulated in this area may have to be used to pay essential bills.
- Presents may have to be limited in this period to ensure essential items of expenditure are paid.

Entertaining
- This category of spending can be reduced dramatically as the payment of essential household bills is more important.
- This is a significantly large proportion of their existing budget and so it may be difficult to reduce spending, but savings will have to be made/reductions in this amount made.

Club memberships
- Unless the memberships are vital, these should at least be suspended, and reinstated when the financial situation improves.
- If the membership is not vital, then it should be stopped and the money diverted to essential bills.

Travel expenses
- If these are work related and are paid back then this may not be a major area of saving.
- If the expenses are not for work and other cheaper means of travel can be used, this should be considered.

Savings
- Whilst it is important to ensure an adequate amount of savings, this may be the time where any savings will have to be used – to meet the needs of essential bills.
- Any savings accumulated in this area may have to be used to pay essential bills.

Mobile phone
- If the mobile phone is not essential, its use should be stopped/limited in order to make some savings.
- If this is a line rental phone, it may be worth considering arranging for the phone to become a pay as you go phone. This means that they can budget for a pre-paid voucher each month and limit use dramatically.
- Ensure that they do not use the phone for outgoing calls as the family will pay for these. The phone can be used for incoming calls only.

Telephone
- A telephone may be important to the family as they have a young child and may need to phone for a doctor. Its use should be greatly reduced/phone at off-peak times.
- They should shop around to see if there is another telephone provider who can offer a cheaper call rate.

Car running costs
- Depending on the location of the new job, Peter could take the bus or walk which would be cheaper.
- If Jade has to be taken to nursery/her grandmother's home, then a bus or walking may be possible to help save money.

Toiletries and household goods
- These can be reduced to only those required for essential cleanliness purposes/household use.
- Many shops offer a 'basics' range of these products which could be purchased at a cheaper price so saving money.

Income
- Jane could take up the offer of extending the number of days that she works. The extra income coming into the house would help the family.
- Peter may get some redundancy money and so might be able to use this to pay some essential bills. This should only be used when other money saving measures have been undertaken.
- The family should look to see if they are entitled to any benefits.

Essential items
Certain essential items will be priority areas for the family:

- mortgage;
- fuel;
- insurance;
- council tax;
- road tax;
- TV license.

as failure to pay these may mean loss of house/legal action.

Only after all of the above changes have been made should the family then begin to look at saving measures in the following areas: food, clothing and house maintenance.

Loans and credit cards
- Loans must be paid and budgeted for – especially as this budget problem is for a limited period.
- Credit card payments should be reduced to the minimum possible for this short period of time.
- If the family are really struggling with payments, contact should be made with the creditors to arrange temporary reduction in payments.
- If the credit cards/loans provide payment protection, this should be investigated as the credit card company may be able to assist the family in meeting their monthly payments.